Austin Allegro

An Enthusiast's Guide

Austin Allegro

An Enthusiast's Guide

Ben Wanklyn

THE CROWOOD PRESS

First published in 2014 by
The Crowood Press Ltd
Ramsbury, Marlborough
Wiltshire SN8 2HR

www.crowood.com

British Library Cataloguing-in-Publication Data
A catalogue record for this book is available from the British Library.

ISBN 978 1 84797 676 5

The Author
Ben Wanklyn is a motoring writer, with a passion for unusual and under-appreciated
classic cars. A freelance writer for *Practical Classics*, *Classic Cars* and *Classic Car Weekly*,
Ben has road-tested a diverse range of classics, dating as far back as the 1920s.
Based in Dorset, he has owned, driven, repaired and had adventures in a number
of Allegros. He currently drives a 1963 Humber Sceptre.

Typeset by Jean Cussons Typesetting, Diss, Norfolk

Printed and bound in Singapore by Craft Print International Ltd

CONTENTS

Acknowledgements   6

Introduction   7

CHAPTER 1   THE CREATION OF THE ALLEGRO: A LEGEND IS BORN   11

CHAPTER 2   THE ALLEGRO SERIES 1, 1973–75: NEW BEGINNINGS   41

CHAPTER 3   THE ALLEGRO 2, 1975–79: GROWING PAINS   70

CHAPTER 4   THE ALLEGRO 3, 1979–82: TWILIGHT YEARS   98

CHAPTER 5   BUYING AND OWNING AN ALLEGRO   127

Index   156

FOR SALLY

ACKNOWLEDGEMENTS

Thanks to: Jenny Thurston, and all the Allegro Club International members who were so kind to offer their assistance; Richard Dredge of Magic Car Pics (www.magiccarpics.co.uk) for his help with sourcing images; Russ Smith, for the action photograph on the cover; Richard Gunn, without whose infectious enthusiasm – and extensive picture collection – this book would not have been possible; my parents and my girlfriend, Sally Eyre, for their unwavering tolerance of my Russet Brown Allegro 3. You were right, Sally…

Much maligned and yet also much loved, no other car is held with as much affection, both despite its failings and because of them.

INTRODUCTION

We love our cars. Of all of the inventions of the twentieth century, no other machine evokes quite the same blend of excitement and emotion as the automobile. But not only do we love great cars, we also have a twisted fascination with bad ones.

To be honest, the Austin Allegro wasn't a particularly bad car. Sure, it looked funny, and the reliability and build-quality troubles weren't great either. It also had the severe misfortune to be built in a time of great industrial unrest, by one of Britain's most troubled car manufacturers. However, it did everything one expected of a car, in a competent manner. Well, most of the time.

The trouble is, no other car in living memory seems to have been branded with such a negative image as the Allegro. For years, it's been a sitting duck, waiting to be pelted with the verbal equivalent of rotten tomatoes. Just read any newspaper

The questionable ergonomics of the infamous quartic steering wheel were legendary. Although awkward to use, its design has become a 1970s icon.

Despite its Marmite styling (you either love it or you hate it), the Allegro was still a functional design. The load-lugging estate variant offered remarkable versatility.

poll on the 'world's worst cars' and see what I mean. In the absence of anything more memorable, the Allegro is an ideal scapegoat for the problems of the British motor industry.

Few put it better than the Allegro's stylist, Harris Mann. 'It took a lot of stick, but it wasn't that bad a car,' he later recalled. 'The trouble was that every one off the line was different in some way, thanks to quality control. I had one as a company car, and it was one of the good ones'.

As a result, few have bothered to explore the little Austin's background; what it was designed to achieve, how it became the way it was, and

what happened to make it so infamous. And what a shame; it's a tale of grand designs, high hopes, management compromises, failed dreams, industrial unrest, national ridicule and, finally, redemption.

Belonging to an era of motoring that has very few survivors at all, the fact that a number of Allegros have endured says something of their ruggedness and the high esteem with which they are held by a loyal band of enthusiasts. Today, many passersby are intrigued, or even delighted, to see such a vehicle from their youth still in active use. Nostalgia is a great healer.

Ignore the 'pig wearing a grille' jibes; the Vanden Plas 1500 was a winner in its niche market sector, thanks to superior trimmings and commendable ride comfort.

When the author was growing up in late 1990s Dorset, Allegros were ten-a-penny. Within a five-minute walk from my house, lived a beige two-door saloon, a Blaze orange estate and a faded 1.7HL Allegro 3, complete with its glorious vinyl roof. What's more, a sighting of a crusty brown Vanden Plas 1500 on its way to the shops, or a red 1300 Super stopped at traffic lights, was no rare occurrence. Allegros were just ordinary cars, to be bought cheaply and driven into the ground.

Despite reasonable longevity, the Allegro's prolonged struggle to pull itself out of banger territory has seen a steady number of them disappear from the roads, forever. Even today, with the little car experiencing something of a comeback as a cheap and cheerful classic, numbers are still dwindling. For the Allegro to fade away, as so many 1970s and 1980s family cars have done, would be to lose a four-wheeled reminder of our motoring history. It's a snapshot of another time, wrapped up in velour and vinyl, and sent bouncing down the road.

With affection and interest increasing every day, it's time that this humble Austin was re-evaluated.

Once it was legendary for being below par, but now, it's simply a legend. No other car has etched itself on to the public consciousness in the same way as the Allegro.

Holding the keys to Austin's most controversial product marks you out as a free-thinking adventurer, yet the Allegro's low cost and economy makes them a sensible classic choice.

CHAPTER ONE

THE CREATION OF THE ALLEGRO: A LEGEND IS BORN

Unveiled on 17 May 1973, the Austin Allegro was unforgettable. However, the story of British Leyland's most infamous product doesn't start there. It owed its very existence to the events that had shaped its creators' fortunes for decades beforehand. To view the Allegro purely as a phenomenon of the 1970s, isolated from the circumstances that led to its conception, is to miss the point. The Allegro's heritage can be traced almost as far back as the dawn of the motor car.

AUSTIN POWERED

The Allegro took its identity from Herbert Austin, one of the pioneers of the British motor industry. The first horseless carriages, powered by internal combustion engines, had appeared in the 1880s,

but by 1895 Austin had built his first car. This three-wheeled machine, with its tiller steering and flat twin engine, owed much to motorcycle technology, as many pioneering motor car designs did. However, it was the start of something big.

As head designer and general manager of the Wolseley Sheep-Shearing Machine Company, Austin developed larger, four-wheeled car designs, which were finally put into production in 1901. Within four years, he had left to start his own company, producing the first Austin car in 1906. From there, the only way was up. A thriving factory was soon producing a wide range of motor cars, varying from 60bhp, 8.7-litre leviathans, all the way down to a modest 6.8bhp offering, named the 'Seven'.

The next Austin to wear the 'Seven' name tag is the best-known today, and started a legacy of

The Allegro may have been very much a product of the 1970s – and has come to symbolize that troubled decade – but it can trace its bloodline through the 1100/1300, Mini and A30, right back to the small Austins of the 1920s.

Where it all started. Although not the first Austin Seven, the 1922 people's car captured the hearts and imaginations of millions of first-time motorists. This 1930s advertisement for the Ruby saloon captures a spirit of adventure that not even the railways could match. BMIHT

small Austins that would endure until the marque disappeared, some seven decades later. Launched in 1922 to compliment the larger 'Twelve', this tiny tourer's aim was to bring many of the features of larger, more expensive cars, within the reach of the aspiring middle-classes.

It succeeded, tempting almost 300,000 owners away from alternatives, such as the motorcycle and sidecar combination. During its seventeen-year lifetime, the baby Austin single-handedly erased the mark left by the cyclecar industry. Its 747cc, water-cooled 4-cylinder engine, and accommodation for two adults and two children, set the benchmark for all small cars that followed. The age of the small, affordable family car had arrived.

CHANGING TIMES

If Austin's early years cemented the firm's reputation as a maker of economical family cars, as well as more exclusive machines, then it was the period following the Second World War that really paved the way for the Allegro. The Seven's successor, the 8, had made way for the all-new, transatlantic-styled Austin A40 Devon and Dorset in 1947. These went some way to gaining sales in valuable markets, such as North America, when the crippled UK economy demanded manufacturers to 'export or die'.

However, the A40 never truly fitted the small-car gap in the range. Something even smaller, and even cheaper, was what the company – now direct-

In the wake of the Second World War, Austin complemented its mid-sized A40 with the new A30 'Seven'. This diminutive machine was frugal, practical and recaptured some of the magic of its earlier namesake. Countryman estates and vans quickly joined the saloons.

By the 1970s, Austin still had its sights fixed on the family motorist. Seaside trips still offered the same sense of freedom, although holidaying on the continent was by now a realistic prospect for the Allegro-owning family.

ed by Leonard Lord following Lord Austin's death in 1941 – desperately needed. What it needed was a new 'Seven'. The car that was unveiled to the world in 1951 was exactly that.

The new A30 'Seven' ticked all of the right boxes with its up-to-date specification. In style, the new saloon was pure 1940s Americana, scaled down for European roads. Although monocoque construction had been only the preserve of brave pioneers, such as André Citroën's Traction Avant, before the war, now it was the becoming the norm, thanks to its weight and cost-savings. Behind the four doors was accommodation for four adults, in addition to a practical-sized boot.

Independent front suspension and a four-speed gearbox were a given, in light of rival Morris' Minor adopting these features upon its 1948 launch. However, where the A30 scored over its rival was with its engine. While the Minor retained a pre-war side-valve unit, the Austin utilized a scaled-down version of the A40's overhead-valve, 4-cylinder powerplant, of 803cc capacity. This was the first incarnation of what would become known as the 'A'-series engine that would eventually find its way into the Allegro.

The A30 was ready for action, just in time for the gradual, yet ultimately relentless, surge in car ownership. As post-war recovery slowly got underway, the 1950s saw more people than ever being able to afford a car, many for the very first time. The practical, yet relatively inexpensive A30 was just the car for the job.

Austin may have been a force to be reckoned with in the marketplace, but its competitors were putting up quite a fight. The Minor, as already mentioned, offered the same values. Ford's new

With room for four in its monocoque body shell, the A30 belonged to a new era of small cars. By the time the revised A35 arrived, shown here, a dramatically improved gearbox was controlled via a shorter, remote gear lever.

Anglia and Prefect 100E models, appearing in 1953, looked even more modern than the Austin and Morris, even if their side-valve engines and three-speed gearboxes were dated. Standard's Eight of the same year was a similarly worthy design, matching the A30's technical specification. However, its spartan, stripped-down nature, and lack of an opening boot-lid, didn't appeal to buyers, prompting rapid introduction of better-equipped versions.

MERGERS AND ACQUISITIONS

Meanwhile, negotiations were under way to merge Austin with the Nuffield Organization, parent company to its greatest competitor, Morris. Such a union had been suggested at several points over the previous decades, but the idea was revived during 1949. On the face of it, the joining of these two old rivals seemed unthinkable. Leonard Lord for one had once been a Morris man, falling out with Lord Nuffield and leaving, before becoming the managing director of Austin. There was a lot of history between the two marques.

However, the benefits of a merger made sense to both sides. Simply becoming a larger company would significantly help both sides to take the turbulence of the hostile car markets on the chin, while the act of pooling resources and integrating overlapping operations would help to streamline such a large organization. With Lord Nuffield and Leonard Lord reconciled, these two industry giants joined forces, forming the British Motor Corporation in July 1952.

By this point, Austin had controlled the Vanden Plas coachworks since 1946. However, the Nuffield Organization brought significantly more marques to the table. Morris was, of course, at the heart of the organization. Lord Nuffield (William Richard Morris) had branched out from motorcycle and bicycle manufacture into motor car manufacture during 1912.

In order to tap into the mass-market, Nuffield kept the cost of his cars low, by farming out component manufacture to numerous small companies in the midlands. Over time, Morris had bought up these firms, simultaneously expanding the company whilst protecting its supply chains. Engines, radiators, transmissions, bodies and even the Skinner's Union (SU) carburettor, were all produced by branches of the Nuffield Organization. In addition, the historic marques of Wolseley and Riley, in addition to the home-grown MG Car Company, also became part of BMC. And so, the new corporation featured no less than six car-manufacturing marques.

MINOR CONCERN

Suddenly, the Austin A30 was thrust into the same model portfolio as its arch rival, the Morris Minor. On the face of it, with two successful models, this significantly strengthened BMC's position within the small-car market. However, with two ranges of cars doing the same job, and competing for the same customers, what would the new company do?

The answer perfectly demonstrated the attitudes present within the newly formed BMC. Both the A30 and Minor were good designs, yet both had significant room for improvement. Focusing on developing and marketing just one of these small cars, whilst slimming down the BMC range, was out of the question.

Loyalties within the marques ran deep, with neither Morris, nor Austin, being able to stomach the thought of playing second fiddle to the other. This was reinforced by BMC's network of dealers. Made up of agents for either Nuffield or Austin, each was fiercely loyal to its own marque. This polarization within the company ran from the separate design studios and factories, all the way to the showroom floor.

As a result, the A30 and Minor continued to compete against one another. It was the same story across the Austin and Morris ranges. However, if streamlining the BMC models was still a step too far, sharing mechanical components went some way to reducing costs and maximizing revenues. The Morris Cowley and Series 2 Oxford used the same 1200 and 1500 B-series engines as the Austin A40 and A50 Cambridges, while the Austin Westminster's C-series engine found its way into the Morris Isis.

Deep beneath the A30's bonnet was a new engine. A scaled-down version of the A40 unit, this 803cc powerplant would eventually become one of the most versatile and long-lived British engines of all time, acquiring the title 'A-series' along the way.

By 1956, the newly developed 948cc version of the A-series engine – along with its much better gearbox – was proving to be a huge improvement over its forerunner. This powerplant transformed the small Austin and Morris into the A35 and Minor 1000. Both had finally matured into class-leading cars, selling strongly with their range of two- and four-door saloons, as well as estate cars and commercial variants (plus a convertible in the case of the Minor). The Minor's underpinnings had even formed the basis for the more powerful and better-equipped Wolseley 1500 and Riley 1.5. With 82,000 A35s sold in 1958, alongside an astonishing 129,000 Minors, BMC's small-car approach was clearly paying off.

The Austin A40 Farina of 1958 was a pro-active move on the part of BMC to keep abreast of the competition. Although mechanically conventional, carrying over the A35's underpinnings, its attractive, modern-looking body shell had been styled by Pininfarina of Italy, adding a touch of glamour to the reliable, yet slightly workaday image of the small Austins.

As the Countryman estate version appeared in 1959, with its innovative horizontally split hatchback, the new Ford Anglia 105E and Triumph Herald appeared, following similar lines of tough, economical underpinnings clothed in attractive bodywork. Meanwhile, the Minor's competence and value meant it was well on its way to becoming the first

One of the A30/ A35's arch rivals was the Morris Minor, also built by BMC. Although slightly larger and heavier, its sure-footedness and good passenger accommodation made it a favourite across the Commonwealth, and even North America, during the 1950s.

British car to sell one million units. The Minor and A40 were proving to be the right cars at the right time, but a revolution was just around the corner. Its name? The Mini.

MINIMALISM

The Suez Crisis of 1956 had seen motorists despair, as petrol prices spiralled ever upwards. Not since wartime rationing had fuel been so scarce, or so expensive. The A35 and the Minor, and even the new A35-derived Austin-Healey 'Frogeye' Sprite, offered commendably good fuel consumption, resulting in a surge in sales. Even so, many were turning to even smaller machines in the quest for ultimate economy.

Minicars, such as the Bond Minicar, Meadows Frisky, Messerschmitt KR175 and BMW's infamous Isetta, were stepping up to the challenge of keeping the less affluent on the roads. With tiny, strangely shaped bodies, and even smaller single- or twin-cylinder engines, their limitations in speed, comfort and practicality were significant. BMC's Leonard Lord saw an opportunity. What he wanted was a rival that could compete with the minicars on running costs, yet offered all the advantages of full-sized cars. With a brief resembling that of the original Austin Seven, he tasked the Minor's creator, Sir Alec Issigonis, with producing such a car.

Appearing in 1959, the result was the Morris Mini-Minor. Simplicity was the watchword of this spacious, box-like little saloon, yet the packaging

The cuddly A35 was revised and re-bodied to create the attractive A40 'Farina' of 1958. With its modern two-box shape and Countryman hatchback option, it was both a frugal family car and a rallying success in the hands of Pat Moss. That is, until the Mini arrived.

used in its design was wholly remarkable. Front-wheel drive was employed, for starters. Although such technology was nothing new, pioneers of the system, such as André Citroën with his Traction Avant, had retained the conventional position of the engine. With a separate gearbox mounted on its end, this resulted in a long nose.

In contrast, the Mini-Minor's engine – a de-stroked 848cc version of the trusty A-series – was turned sideways, to sit across the front of the vehicle. This in turn meant that there was no room to mount a conventional gearbox on to the end of the engine. Issigonis' extraordinary solution was to locate the transmission within the engine's sump, sharing the same oil. From there, power was delivered to the front wheels by drive-shafts and CV joints. The result was that, of the car's 10ft (3m) overall length, almost 80 per cent was devoted to passengers and their luggage.

The rest of the design was also a space-saving masterpiece. Rubber cones replaced conventional springs within the suspension, with the tiny 10-inch wheels placed right at the corners of the vehicle. Sliding door glass freed up elbow and storage room within the hollow doors, and four full-sized passengers could hide their possessions in any number of storage cubbies, shelves and bins. A satisfying side-effect of such minimalist design was incredible road-holding, ensuring the Mini-Minor was a delight to drive.

Morris' fervent dealer network had demanded their version of the new car first, yet an Austin-badged version followed soon afterwards, in 1960. By reviving the historic 'Seven' title from the now-deceased A30/A35 range, it was clear that this was the latest spiritual successor to Austin's original people's car.

Although retrospectively regarded as a roaring success, conservative buyers were initially scared off by such radical modernism. BMC's way of

Sir Alec Issigonis (pictured) changed the small-car game with his Mini. Ultra-compact packaging and front-wheel drive set the bar high for all other small cars, suddenly making BMC's other, conventional designs look rather old hat.

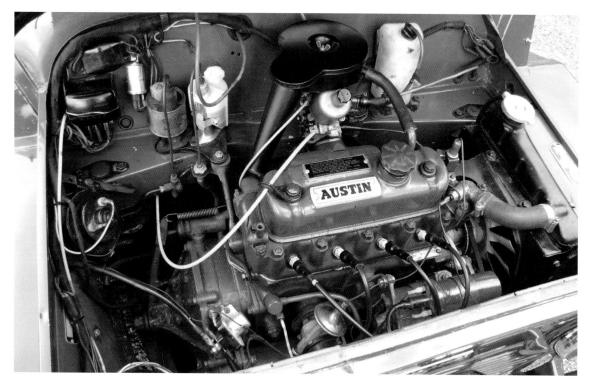

Front-wheel drive was nothing new, but Issigonis' masterstroke was to turn the A-series engine sideways and squeeze the transmission into its sump. This space-saving magic eventually saw the creation of a four-speed automatic derivative – an astonishing feat.

combating this was to sell the Mini as a loss-leader – a fact that only came to light when arch-rivals Ford disassembled one and worked out how much it cost to produce.

As a result, with the new decade, Mini sales snowballed, with the chic little car becoming a cultural icon during the process. Beloved by actors, royalty, film stars, rally drivers and pensioners alike, its own functional style made it a 'classless' car, breaking down social boundaries with its universal appeal.

Within a few short years, a perplexing variety of Minis was on offer. Handy vans and pick-ups were complemented by the stripped-down, utilitarian Moke, while a selection of fiery Cooper and Cooper 'S' models built on the Mini's motorsport success. The Riley Elf and Wolseley Hornet added traditional grilles, a larger boot and plush trimmings, to move the car upmarket.

POPULARITY CONTEST

However, for every Mini that was sold during the 1960s, BMC was managing to sell two examples of its larger sibling: the 1100. From a commercial viewpoint, this was the real breakthrough for BMC, and the car that the Allegro directly owed its existence to. Issigonis had been tasked with penning an all-new family saloon, based on the same principles as the Mini, which would bring the same space-saving, good-handling design virtues to a much larger sector of the British car-buying public. This project had been given the designation Austin Design Office (ADO) 16.

Whereas the Mini's appearance had been a direct result of its uncompromising construction, this larger car had been given clean, crisp lines by Pininfarina, resulting in a thoroughly modern appearance. Inside the spacious body shell, there

The Mini would prove to be one of BMC's greatest successes, appealing to all classes and all pockets. Within a few short years, this radical car was not only a cheap urban runabout but a chic fashion accessory, as well as a serious rallying tool. BMIHT

While the Mini grabbed the headlines, BMC shrewdly offered its technology in a slightly larger, family-friendly design. The Morris 1100 of 1962 proved to be just what the British public wanted, offering astonishing interior space, while also being a hoot to drive. BMIHT

was much more room for four, or even five, passengers, thanks to a longer wheelbase. The interior space, on a par with that offered by far larger cars, was truly staggering for one that was only 12ft (3.5m) long. There was also a reasonably sized boot, while beneath the bonnet lay the familiar A-series engine, stretched to a new 1098cc capacity. As with the Mini, this drove the front wheels, through a four-speed gearbox.

Gone were the rubber cones that had suspended the corners of the Mini. In their place was a new system, devised by suspension specialist Dr Alex Moulton. The springing medium was still rubber, but the damping of shocks was done hydraulically. Each side of the car was connected from front to rear by pipes, filled with fluid. As the front corner of the car hit a bump and the suspension was compressed, this would increase the pressure of the fluid in the rear corner on that side, keeping the car riding level. The same effect would happen to the front corner, when its rear counterpart was compressed. This whole assembly was mounted on the front and rear sub-frames.

Named 'Hydrolastic', this smooth new suspension

The 1100 was swiftly offered in many guises. Alongside the basic Morris and Austin were a plusher Wolseley, a sportier MG, plus the all-bells-and-whistles Riley Kestrel, as shown here. An even more extravagant Vanden Plas Princess variant was unveiled in 1963.

system was a huge leap forward over the traditional mechanical springing systems used in the older Minor and A40. It gave the little car a commendably good ride, even if pitching backwards and forwards could occur under extreme conditions. The marketing tag-lines were – astonishingly for advertisement copy – completely correct in their descriptions of the 'float on fluid' ride. Hydrolastic would quickly find its way into the Mini, too.

The Morris 1100, as this smart new saloon was called, appeared in showrooms in 1962. BMC were well and truly on the money with the ADO16 design. With practicality, economy and surprisingly good driving dynamics – despite the upright steering column angle, which it shared with the Mini – the 1100 was exactly the right car at the right time. Even up against Ford's more glamorous, yet conventionally engineered rival, the Cortina, the little Morris was a hugely attractive proposition for countless buyers.

Sales were strong from the outset, prompting the introduction of a number of different variants. Wearing an upright MG-style grille, the MG 1100 gave friskier performance with its twin carburettors and improved cylinder head. A basic Austin version joined the range in 1963, followed swiftly by a plusher Wolseley variant, plus the bells-and-whistles Riley Kestrel 1100. The Vanden Plas Princess 1100 was the luxurious conclusion of the car's badge-engineered derivatives.

LAND LUBBER

From the second-best selling car in Britain in 1963, the 1100 had occupied the top spot by the following year. The Cortina, which now occupied the number 2 position, was giving the ADO16 design a run for its money, though. Competitive pricing, more equipment, bigger engine options and added glamour from motorsport success, all made the Ford a deadly rival. The 1100 out-sold the Cortina through 1965 and 1966, aided by the introduction of Austin and Morris estate car versions, before being finally overtaken by the Ford, now into its second incarnation.

As luck would have it, BMC had just developed a new version of the A-series engine, using the 1275cc capacity already seen on some versions of the Mini Cooper 'S'. With this pokier powerplant installed in the ADO16 nose, the 1300 was created. Selling alongside the existing 1100, this was enough to put the popular small-car design back on top in the Ford–BMC sales war. From 1968, up until 1972, the 1100/1300 was the best-selling car in the UK, being built at both the Longbridge and Cowley production plants. BMC were perhaps not far from the truth when they heralded it as 'the British people's car'.

Meanwhile, Issigonis had a third trick up his sleeve. After the success of the Mini and the 1100/1300, it was high time that BMC's larger, mid- to large-sized family car category contenders were given a good work over. The 'family' Farina range of large saloons and estates had been fulfilling this role up until now.

As with the 1100/1300, a confusing number of different marque identities had been applied to essentially the same car, resulting in the Austin A60 Cambridge and Morris Oxford Series VI versions being supplemented by the Wolseley 16/60, the Riley 4/72 and the MG Magnette Mk IV. Tough, reliable and competent, these models were good money earners for the corporation. However, this middle-aged design was also starting to lag behind the times, with underpinnings set up for comfort, rather than performance.

TWO OUT OF THREE

BMC's solution was the 1800. Again available initially as a Morris, then as an Austin and finally as the upmarket Wolseley 18/85, this extended the Mini's basic engineering principles even further. A 1798cc B-series 4-cylinder engine was mounted transversely, driving the front wheels through a four-speed gearbox, while Hydrolastic suspension cushioned the large monocoque body shell from the road surface below.

As with the 1100, Pininfarina was drafted in to bring a little flair into the styling. Sadly, this was not as successful an attempt as with the smaller saloon. Although not ugly, the results were a little awkward from certain angles. A wide, grinning front grille didn't help matters. Still, there was no denying

Next size up in Issigonis' new range was the 1800/2200 range, available as an Austin, Morris or Wolseley. Tough, good to drive and incredibly spacious, its odd appearance and minimalist trimmings drove many buyers into the arms of Rootes, Ford, Vauxhall and others. BMIHT

the staggering amount of space that was on offer within; in terms of passenger accommodation, the 1800 was in a league of its own

What's more, like its smaller siblings, the new car possessed both a comfortable ride and keen road-holding. Such was this big car's Mini-like chuck-ability that it went on to become a long-distance rallying favourite, acquiring the 'landcrab' nickname for its sideways antics. In the gruelling, 7,000-mile, London–Sydney Marathon of 1968, Paddy Hop-kirk's Austin 1800 took second place. Impressive, considering that only fifty-six of the seventy-two competitors managed to finish at all.

Interestingly, the big Austin/Morris 1800 proved to be particularly successful in Australia, where its performance and rugged design made it a winner against the home-grown Holdens and

Fords. The 1800 was eventually joined by Ley-land Australia's own Kimberly and Tasman deriva-tives, which were tailored exclusively to satisfy Australian tastes.

However, in the UK, things were less rosy for the big car. Issigonis' space-saving ideals, which had revolutionized the small-car world, were less important to the buyers of larger cars. Plush trim-mings, equipment options and exciting engines were of greater concern to them; qualities that the far more stylish Fords and Vauxhalls offered. The 1800's plain, featureless interior just wasn't what buyers expected.

Just as the Austin A40 and Morris Minor had continued in production as low-tech, bargain alter-natives to the 1100/1300, so the 'family' Farinas had soldiered on after the introduction of the 1800. This

The 1300 was launched in 1967, continuing the ADO16 range's phenomenal success. By this point, two- and four-door saloons were available, as well as the Countryman estate. However, by the time the last 1300 was built in 1974, the small-car world had moved on. BMIHT

was just as well, as the 1800 just wasn't a success. Even the addition of the 6-cylinder Austin/Morris 2200 and Wolseley Six in 1972 couldn't change this. Over its eleven-year life, little more than 386,000 examples of the 1800/2200 were sold. This proved that the familiar layout of BMC's front-wheel-drive saloons wasn't necessarily a guaranteed route to success.

LEYLAND LIFE

By the mid-1960s, it was becoming clear that BMC was in an increasingly perilous situation, with its profitability rapidly slipping away. Successes, such as the ADO16 range, had been countered by flops, like the larger 1800. The bold intentions that had existed at BMC's creation in 1952, to streamline and rationalize the mighty empire of factories, brands and designs, had only been semi-successful. In relation to its output and in comparison to more efficient rivals, BMC, with over 200,000 employees, was still significantly overstaffed.

What's more, many of its designs were ageing rapidly, urgently requiring huge investment to replace or rejuvenate. Machines such as the Austin A60 Cambridge and Morris Minor 1000 belonged to a different era, and just couldn't keep

The poor old Marina had its hands tied thanks to compromises in its engineering, yet its smart, roomy body and decent specification meant it was a key money-earner for BL, appealing as a conventional, good-value alternative to the front-wheel-drive Austins.

Filling the chasm in the middle of the Austin range, the Maxi of 1969 was Issigonis' last hurrah. Not even penny-pinching sharing of the 1800's doors could detract from its spacious and versatile hatchback design. Sadly, early reliability woes damaged its prospects. BMIHT

up with ever-changing competition. The diminishing profitability of many of its products meant that there was less money being stretched across the sprawling organization. Something had to be done.

To make matters worse, this was an unsteady time for car manufacturers across Europe. Marques were joining forces for strength and safety amid a hostile climate, or were being taken over, brought under state control or collapsing altogether. In Britain, Standard–Triumph had merged first with Leyland commercial vehicles in 1963, then Rover (including Land-Rover and Alvis) four years later. The mighty Rootes Group had been under the ownership of Chrysler since 1964, while the likes of Ford and Vauxhall were already offshoots of American companies.

Seeking stability, BMC joined with Jaguar and Daimler, along with the Pressed Steel body manufacturing firm, to create British Motor Holdings in 1966. However, the newly-formed BMH still had many problems, and the situation was only going to get tougher. With stretched funds, the increasingly troubled company entered into negotiations to form an even greater organization.

Leyland looked like a good bedfellow for the ailing BMH. Its successful truck-manufacturing operations were now complemented by its portfolio of quality, higher priced cars, courtesy of Rover, Jaguar, Daimler and Triumph. Keen to avoid BMH's collapse, and the black hole that would have created at the heart of Britain's manufacturing base, Harold Wilson's Labour Government was particularly keen for such a merger. The Ministry of Technology stepped in to aid the formation of a deal, and in January 1968 it was announced that BMH and Leyland would join forces. The British Leyland Motor Corporation had been created.

MERGE IN TURN

When the agreed merger took place in May of that year, the newly formed BL found itself looking after a dozen car marques alone, alongside bus and commercial vehicle concerns, engineering and component manufacturers, and a whole host of supplementary businesses. It was Britain's biggest industrial organization, and one that had the potential to produce over one million vehicles per year, from its numerous production facilities.

However, this increase in size hadn't helped what was once BMH. After all, many of its problems were caused by its unwieldy, costly nature. Organization was needed to ensure the new company's survival, so BL was split into seven sections. Austin Morris was the first, taking care of the lower cost yet commercially vital saloons and estates of those two brands.

The remainder of car manufacturing came under the Specialist Cars' umbrella, offering more exclusive marques that retailed for higher prices. Interestingly, this also included Triumph, whereas its once-arch rival MG was now a part of the Austin Morris sector; the latter's role was clearly as a maker of affordable sports cars. Five more categories divided up the Construction Equipment, Pressed Steel and Fisher (incorporating the Pressed Steel and Ludlow Fisher body shell plants), Trucks

and Buses, Foundry and General Engineering and, lastly, the Overseas department.

Make no mistake, BL was vast. At its head was former BMH premier George Harriman, although his tenure was cut short due to ill health. So, within six months, Leyland's managing director Donald Stokes took the reins as chairman. He was joined by George Turnbull, the new managing director of Austin Morris, as well as Harry Webster as technical director; both had come from Leyland. With new leaders for the new corporation, one of the first tasks was to shake up the lower end of the new BL range.

HATCHING A PLAN

During the BMC years, Austin and Morris had gone from sharing key components on their models,

An all-new, overhead camshaft engine was commissioned to power the new Maxi. Labelled the E-series, its original 1485cc capacity was soon stretched to 1748cc, also spawning a 6-cylinder variant. It soon became the beating heart of most of the Allegro range.

Minimal funding called for frugal face-lifts. The Maxi-esque snout of the Mini Clubman was a success, but this hatchback-devoid design was starting to lag behind the superminis of the 1970s, such as the Renault 5 and Volkswagen Polo.

such as engines and transmissions, to offering what were in effect re-badged versions of the same cars. On designs such as the Mini, only the grille pattern and badges distinguished the Morris version from its Austin equivalent. What these two marques needed was, in this new BL era, to regain their separate brand identities. Rather than offering the same product, both would instead try to appeal to different groups of car buyers.

Morris would become a purveyor of sensible, no-nonsense family cars, offering sound value for money. Conventional mechanicals would be the order of the day – an approach that was serving Ford, Vauxhall and Chrysler UK very well indeed. Practicality and space were more important that trend-setting design concepts.

Austin, on the other hand, had a much more ambitious role mapped out for it. This would be the brand to carry forward the torch of technical progress that the Issigonis models of the 1960s had ignited. With front-wheel drive, advanced suspension systems and the clever use of interior space, Austin would continue to prove to the world that innovation could be made to work on affordable, mass-produced cars. This was a brave, yet very worthwhile, path for the historic marque to tread.

With this in mind, it was decided that an unfinished car design that BL had inherited would become purely an Austin. On the face of it, this 1.5-litre car ticked all of the right boxes. A big, spacious body, suspended by Hydrolastic suspension, and driven by front-wheel drive, was powered by an all-new overhead camshaft engine and a five-speed gearbox. What's more, in addition to four doors, a hatchback was provided; this was a multi-purpose estate car in the mould of the revolutionary Renault 16. At the head of this project was a familiar face; Sir Alec Issigonis.

After the 1800 had failed to leave much of a mark, it was decided that its design had been too big and too powerful, having moved too far beyond its original target. Issigonis had set about designing a car that was more in-touch with buyers' demands. However, by the time that this second-chance project had come under the influence of BL, compromises had been made.

Although the designing of an all-new engine and transmission had been approved, George Harriman had made the cost-reducing decision to carry over the 1800's doors on to the new car. As a result, the design had to be tweaked to accommodate these old items, damaging its all-new appearance in the process.

What's more, the cable-operated gear-change for the new transmission was proving troublesome, while the car's limited power and underwhelming style worried the BL management. However, it was much too late to start again; after a flurry of revisions, the new car hit the road in May 1969, named the Maxi – a logical step up from the Mini.

Finally, the A60 Cambridge was laid to rest and the new Maxi stepped up to take its place. Its plus points were numerous, with the good ride, handling and interior space that characterized Issigonis' designs, plus the novel feature of seats that folded flat to create a bed. Sadly, its odd looks, high price and poor gear-change snatched defeat from the jaws of victory, resulting in initially sluggish sales.

A hasty re-launch in 1970 included a whole host of improvements, not least a more positive rod gear-change mechanism and the option of a longer stroke 1750 engine. These boosted the Maxi's popularity considerably, although sales never quite matched the hopes of BL. With 486,273 examples sold over an eleven-year lifetime, the Maxi had followed in the footsteps of the 1800 before it, and failed to live up to sales expectations.

NEW DRIVING FORCE

By this point, Austin Morris was still relying heavily on the old ADO16 design. Although its continued success as the number one selling car in Britain was welcome, it was a situation that couldn't last forever. The 1100/1300 may have been a winner, but as it aged, its design limitations became more and more obvious.

The almost boat-like pitching of its suspension on very rough roads was a concern, as was its limited boot space, uncomfortably upright driving position and styling, which had barely changed since 1962. What's more, its inability to offer more than 1275cc and four gears was a drawback, when Ford's Cortina rival was getting larger and more luxurious with every new generation.

The trouble was that, despite its flaws, the 1100/1300 was still both likeable and popular. Any intended replacement would have to re-create its combination of sure-footed handling, space efficiency and, ultimately, charm; a hard act to follow. BL set to work on a direct replacement. Replicating the old car's front-wheel-drive layout was a prior-

Better traction on corners and slippery roads.

With an engine bay designed to accommodate both A- and E-series engines, there was at least plenty of room to work on the powerplant. This cutaway model displays the new suspension system developed for the Allegro: Hydragas. BMIHT

As work started on the ADO16 replacement, Harris Mann sketched this lithe, shark-nosed little car. Note the low bodywork and deep, steeply raked windscreen. This handsome machine didn't make it to the production line without serious compromises.

ity from the outset, which in turn meant that the new model, code-named ADO67, would have to be marketed purely as an Austin – the new brand identities demanded it.

While plans for a new Austin were being discussed, BL had been working overtime to put its new Morris into production. The lack of a truly competitive mid-sized family car design meant that the corporation was missing out, in a market where there was everything to gain. What's more, Morris' range was decidedly long in the tooth; the old 'family' Farina Oxford Series VI was still battling on, outmoded and long out of date. BL, however, had a quick-fix solution to replace it.

Ex-Ford stylist Roy Haynes, who had previously styled the Ford Cortina Mk2, penned a smart-looking four-door saloon, along with an attractive two-door coupé. These new body shells were given a modern, well-equipped interior, plus the option of the hardy 1.8-litre B-series engine or the plucky 1.3-litre A-series powerplant. This new car, named the Morris Marina, appeared in showrooms across the UK in double-quick time.

On paper, the new car was exactly the kind of conventional, good-value car that Morris needed to be offering in 1971. Unfortunately, there was a problem. In an effort to speed up development and lower costs, the old Minor's underpinnings had been carried on to the new car. This mix of front torsion bars, lever arm dampers and rear leaf-springs had worked well in the past and was beefed up for its new role.

However, this old technology simply wasn't up to the job. With much more weight on board, the new car suffered badly from under-steer, particularly in the nose-heavy 1.8. Severe press criticism of this surprising handling defect spurred BL to carry out rapid suspension revisions, but by then, the damage had been done. The name of another new Austin Morris car had been blackened, before it had even had a chance to start selling. This meant that the stakes were even higher for the proposed new Austin. It simply had to be successful; there was no other option.

MULTI-PURPOSE

The failure of the Maxi and Marina to make much of a splash in the mid-sized family car market had a knock-on effect with the intended 1100/1300 replacement. Instead of simply stepping into the shoes of the older car, the brief for the ADO67 was changing rapidly. As George Turnbull described in 1973, 'We wanted to produce a car which would be all things to all men. As we saw it, we wanted a medium sized family car, with advanced engineering features, good performance, exceptional comfort, road-holding, steering; in fact, a personal car.'

This concept for a 'personal car' meant that the new Austin would have to be a lot more than just an 1100/1300 replacement. Broadening the car's appeal would mean increasing the range of engines beyond the traditional 1100 and 1300 capacities.

By this point, the styling was already coming on apace. A promising designer, who had originally joined BMC from Ford along with Roy Haynes, was heading up the new car's appearance. Harris Mann was his name, and his sleek ADO67 design proposal had been chosen by management from a selection of five during 1969.

The car that Mann had envisaged was an impressive-looking machine. Low and sleek, its rakish body featured a low waistline, as the old 1100/1300 had done, which in turn gave a large glass area. The front and rear windscreens were steeply angled in an aerodynamic fashion, while at the front of the car, a dramatic shark-nose prow was used.

HARRIS MANN

To the casual observer, Harris Mann was the architect of some of the most challenging car designs of the 1970s. The Allegro, Princess and TR7 all owe their designs to him, while he was also involved in the Marina and Ital, in addition to the Maestro and Metro.

Born in 1938, Mann grew up with a deep fascination with automotive design. Following training at engineering school, he served his apprenticeship with the coach and bus builder Duple. From there, he worked for the legendary Raymond Loewy Company in America, before returning to the UK to serve his national service. Working again for Duple, before the Commer commercial vehicles section of the Rootes Group, Mann moved to Ford in 1962 as a feasibility engineer.

With an impressive design portfolio, Mann quickly moved to Ford's design studios at Averley and Dunton. This was an exciting time to be part of Ford UK. The company's drive to inject glamour and desirability into its products had already spawned the Cortina MkI, Anglia 105E and Zephyr and Zodiac Mk3 range, to name but a few. Very soon, Mann found himself as part of the team working on two stylish new car designs: the Escort MkI and the Capri MkI.

By this point, Mann was working beneath Ford of Europe's chief exterior stylist, Roy Haynes, who had also designed the Cortina Mk2. When Haynes was head-hunted by BMC in 1967, to start a new studio at Morris' Cowley plant, Mann went with him. However, with design mavericks such as Alec Issigonis and Dick Burzi ruling the roost within the corporation, BMC proved to be less forward-thinking and a lot less welcoming than Ford had been. 'When you looked around at what the rest of Europe was doing, BMC was like a mausoleum,' Mann later recalled.

As Haynes pieced together the ADO28 project, which became the Marina, Mann was heavily involved. However, corporation in-fighting muddied the relationship between the Cowley studio and its Longbridge-based equivalent. When Haynes tired of such politics and left, Mann was moved across to Longbridge.

However, Mann had already been experimenting with radical new ideas, with the wedge-shaped Zanda sports car. 'In the back of my mind, I saw that as the route MG should take,' recalled Mann. 'I thought they should look at mid-engined designs. It was my way of tickling management.' This showcase of Mann's talents helped him to secure the position of chief designer on what was to become the Allegro.

Although the ADO67 end-product was far removed from Mann's original intentions, his next project, codenamed Diablo, was far purer in its final design. Hitting the road in 1975, the radical wedge-shaped Princess was a bold and forward-looking design, even though BL politics had stripped it of its proposed hatchback to avoid competition with the Maxi and the forthcoming Rover SD1. 'It was a boo-boo,' Mann explains. 'By the time the Ambassador came along, with a hatchback, it was all too late.'

Mann's Triumph TR7 again followed the wedge concept, with its streamlined nose and pop-up headlamps. This civilized design was the right car for the times, and was rewarded with good sales. Next came the miniMetro of 1980, which Mann played a part in shaping, before assisting with Rover stylist David Bache's Maestro project. Finally, in 1983, Mann left the in-fighting BL for freelance work with other firms. Since then, he has designed Channel Tunnel trains, trucks and even helped re-style the Subaru Impreza, before helping with MG-Rover's SV sports car. Today, he is a university lecturer on design.

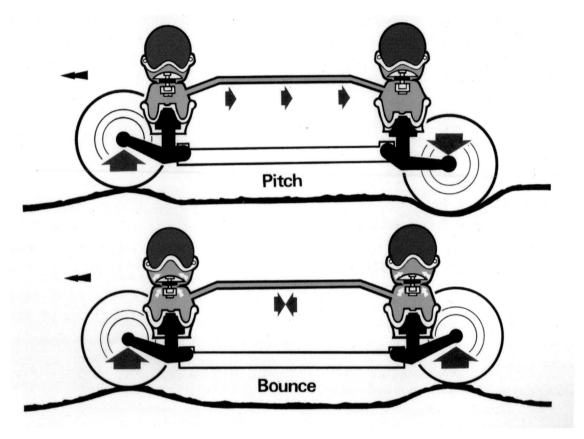

Designed by Alex Moulton to improve on the old Hydrolastic suspension, Hydragas consisted of gas-filled spheres on each corner, connected front to rear by pipes of fluid. As one wheel was pushed up by a bump, its opposing number was pushed down to compensate. BMIHT

The result was a dramatic and distinctive-looking saloon car; Harris Mann had conceived something that looked rather exciting.

However, from this promising start, compromises started to be made to the design at a corporate level. Technical director Harry Webster recalled that 'the styling boys had a completely clean sheet of paper to start with, and I had a good deal of freedom on the engineering side'. However, the engineering side would quickly start to interfere with the ADO67's appearance, ensuring that the 'clean sheet' wasn't so clean after all.

To save costs, it was decreed that the heater from the Marina would be fitted to the new Austin. According to Mann, this was developed 'at astronomical cost… that had to go in'. The sheer bulki-

ness of this unit in turn dictated that the bulkhead's height should be raised, reducing the design's sleek effect.

Then the real killer-blow to the car's style came. The decision to expand the car's range of engines had led to compromises. The Maxi's 1500 and 1750 engines, designated the E-series, were being built by the new, purpose-built Cofton Hackett engine plant. However, with underwhelming sales of the Maxi, there was a huge excess capacity that needed to be exploited, in order to regain some of BL's colossal investment in the new plant. Ensuring that the ADO67 used the E-series would kill two birds with one stone, providing the required engine capacities while making up for the Maxi's underperformance.

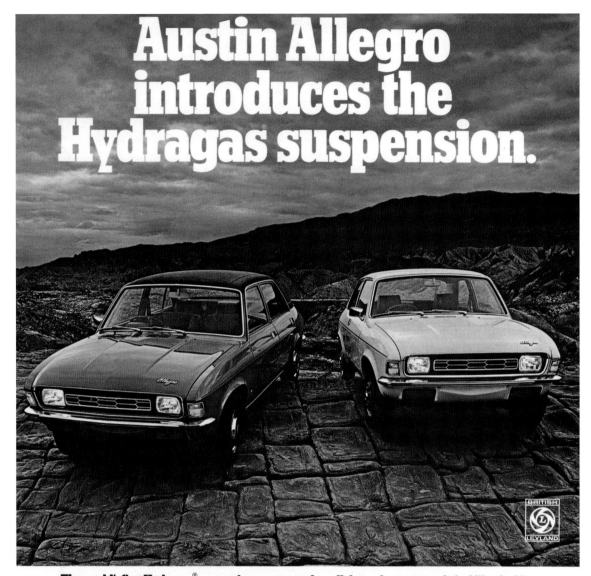

Austin Allegro introduces the Hydragas suspension.

The world's first Hydragas® suspension system makes all those short-cut roads feel like the M1.

Sometimes you may like to get off the beaten track.

Take those short-cut roads that other cars just have to avoid.

That's when the rugged character of the Allegro and a revolutionary suspension system called Hydragas® really come into their own.

Hydragas® is a revolutionary suspension that rides on gas. It gives Allegro far superior handling qualities to any other car in its price range.

It's a tough system too because it needs no regular maintenance for the life of the car.

We drove a test car over a high kerb at 30 mph more than 1,000 times to prove it.

Combine that with the extra traction of front-wheel drive and you've got a car that's a pure delight to handle.

Safer too, on corners and wet roads.

Allegro gives you a power choice from 1100 to 1750 plus a five speed gearbox on all 1500 and 1750 models – and that's a feature never before offered in a range of this type.

An electric cooling fan which aids engine efficiency and front disc brakes.

A Quartic steering wheel that's shaped to let you see your instruments more clearly and give you more positive control.

Room for 5 people and 15 cu. ft. of boot space. Alternator. Fresh-flow ventilation. Comprehensive safety package.

And there are 12 models to choose from, starting at the 2-door 1100 DeLuxe all the way along to the powerful 4-door 1750 Sport Special.

Pick one out at your Austin dealer now, before the waiting list builds up.

Allegro
The new driving force from Austin.

RECOMMENDED PRICES FROM £973.59 INC CAR TAX AND VAT.
DELIVERY CHARGES, SEAT BELTS AND NUMBER PLATES EXTRA.

Similar in effect to Citroën's hydraulic suspension systems, Hydragas' smoothness and bump absorption was the Allegro's biggest selling point. As the system was improved, it became a worthy system, later fitted to the Princess, Metro, MGF and retro-fitted to the Hydrolastic Maxi. BMIHT

HIGH RIDER

When this decision was translated on to the drawing board, problems started to arise. Unlike the diminutive A-series, the new engine and transmission were incredibly tall. However, there was no money available to develop a more compact power unit, with Webster firmly stating that 'there was no question of any major revision on the mechanical side'. With the design team's hands tied, the existing concept had to be made to accept this engine.

'We had to put in the E-series engine,' explained Mann, 'which was more suitable for putting in a Leyland truck. So, the car gained in height. This made it look shorter and stumpier.' As the body was stretched and teased to accommodate cast-off Maxi and Marina components, the design's sleekness went out of the window.

'Once these new requirements started to come in, the height went up, the body got a little bit more bloated, and from our original concepts we created in the studio, they weren't able to be achieved any more,' Mann described. 'I think the specification, which we'd been dictated to, didn't allow us to really regenerate a new 1100.' When later asked how he felt about the way the ADO67 project ultimately ended up looking, Mann simply said, 'disappointed, really'.

As far as BL management was concerned, this new Austin didn't have to look all that impressive. Fashionable styling wasn't a requirement on a forward-thinking, technically innovative car. After all, the likes of Citroën and Renault were renowned for producing market-leading cars that didn't follow contemporary trends. However, there were concerns from other parts of the organization that the new car just didn't look right. The Range Rover's designer, Spen King, described it as looking 'like a caricature of Henry VIII, with little features and a big, bulging face'.

As if to make matters worse, it was decreed that the new Austin should feature a square steering wheel – an unusual feature. 'That came from engineering,' said Mann. 'It wasn't very good at all. But we were instructed to do it.' The logic behind this addition was that it would reflect the car's quirky and ultra-modern image. Stylistically, there may

MAXI AND THE E-SERIES

The larger two capacities of Allegro powerplant were variations on the British Leyland E-series engine. Like the A-, B- and C-series corporate designs before it, the E-series was destined to be used in a selection of different vehicles. However, its development was intertwined with that of the Maxi, the last entire car design that Sir Alec Issigonis would steer through to production.

The Maxi was conceived to take over from the outdated, yet still profitable, Austin, Morris and Wolseley 'family' Farina saloons. The 1800 of 1964 had already failed to achieve this objective, so work started on an all-new design, incorporating many of the design trademarks of its creator: front-wheel drive, a transverse engine, impressive interior space efficiency, plus Alex Moulton's well-proven Hydrolastic suspension system.

Sir Alec had envisaged a small-capacity four, capable of being enlarged to a sub 2-litre straight-six for use in other models. However, with the weight of the new car rapidly increasing, thanks to the use of the 1800's doors, a mere 1300cc capacity would have been insufficient. Instead,

George Harriman, BMC's managing director, gave the go-ahead for a larger overhead camshaft engine to be designed.

The result was the E-series. Although not a lightweight powerplant, due to its iron engine block and cylinder head, its intention was to be as rugged and dependable as the engine designs that had preceded it. Boasting a single overhead camshaft, this was a more modern and sophisticated design than the ancient A- and B-series, with their side-mounted cams and push rods. Intended for use with front-wheel-drive transmissions, a new five-speed gearbox was developed to complement this power unit.

Launched in the Maxi in May 1969, in a 1485cc capacity, the E-series produced a reasonable 74bhp. However, in the heavy Maxi, this was a little underwhelming. Unfortunately, there were greater concerns from its matching gearbox. It rapidly became apparent that the cable-operated gear-change simply didn't work properly. Even after frantic pre-launch adjustments, selecting gears was still an unpleasant business, prompting the now-legendary references to 'stirring a bag of marbles with a knitting needle' comments from the motoring press.

A rod-change gearbox in 1970 helped matters somewhat, swiftly followed by a four-speed automatic transmission from Automotive Products. Although the E-series' potential for capacity enlargement was limited, lengthening the piston stroke boosted its size to 1749cc, giving 84bhp in single-carb form and 95bhp with twin carburettors and a higher compression ratio. The latter was used in the upmarket HL Maxi.

Meanwhile, this engine was being put to work in Australia. The old 1100/1300 four-door saloon was given a useful hatchback and the 1500 engine, to become the Morris Nomad. What's more, Leyland Australia turned the engine round by 90 degrees and used it in their own version of the rear-wheel-drive Marina. The E-series made it competitive against Japanese and home-grown competitors.

The original 6-cylinder concept didn't die, though. The 2227cc E6 engine, as used in the 2200 ADO17 'Landcrab', was based heavily on the E-series design, later powering the 6-cylinder Princess models. In Australia, this unit was used in the 2200-based Austin Kimberley, as well as the unique Leyland P76 saloon and the racy Marina 'Red Six'. The last E6 was used in the Ambassador in 1982, while the E-series was finally developed into the Maestro's 1598cc R-series, and then the S-series, which survived until 1993.

The Allegro's ability to tackle rough ground and poor surfaces was remarkable, although some bumps were still too big.

have been missed opportunities with the ADO67 design, but there were exciting developments happening in other aspects of its design.

LIFE'S A GAS

Alex Moulton, whose Hydrolastic suspension had given the BMC/BL front-wheel-drive designs exemplary ride and cornering qualities, had already been working to improve the system. An extensive re-design aimed to maintain its stability, soft ride and ruggedness, while ironing out the pitching and wallowing flaws. Donald Stokes wanted Moulton's new and improved suspension to be incorporated into the ADO67 project. Following a rigorous programme of testing and development, the results were exciting.

Instead of the all-fluid arrangement used in the Hydrolastic suspension system, with rubber providing the springing, the latest development of the concept would also incorporate gas into its construction. Named Hydragas, metal spheres of nitrogen were compressed by the suspension arms, taking the job of conventional springs. This gas was separated from the fluid by rubber diaphragms, with pipes connecting the front and rear corners of the car as before. Just like with Hydrolastic, the system's ability to stay level on rough ground was remarkable, although the gas springing provided a new level of flexibility.

Predictably, radial tyres were the only option for the ADO67. However, thanks to the versatility of its new suspension, these only needed to be relatively slender; the wheels would stay planted on

If the Allegro was disappointingly compromised, the larger Princess was much closer to Harris Mann's ideal. Its class-leading comfort and dramatic looks made it a revolutionary design, although BL management snubbed Mann's hatchback at the last minute. BMIHT

the tarmac without the use of wider wheel rims. The wheels were increased in size to 13 inches in diameter, as opposed to the 12-inch units of the 1100/1300.

Meanwhile, the dimensions of the car were being increased yet again. At the front, the engine bay was made longer, to accommodate a front-mounted radiator. Although a simple feature, this solved several problems with the old 1100/1300 design. More efficient than the side-mounted versions fitted to the previous generation of front-wheel drive BMC/BL cars, this incorporated a thermostatically operated electrical fan.

Not only did this free up power lost by driving a mechanical fan, it made the running engine much quieter. With European drive-by noise regulations on the horizon, this was a smart move. A positive side-effect was to reduce the potential for the engine's front-mounted distributor to become soaked in wet weather.

Extra thought was put into protecting the car's occupants in the event of a collision – a consideration that hadn't been made during the outgoing model's conception. Harry Webster explained in 1973 that:

> ... my people had to think of the safety regulations, both actual and proposed. In our new car the length from toe board to rear seat is exactly the same as in a 1300: the extra few inches have gone partly into the boot and partly, together with radiator, into the nose, so as to provide just that little bit of extra crushability in an accident. The extra width, similarly, is in the doors, leaving room for some more side-impact protection.

READY TO ROLL

With scrutiny directed to the car's prototypes, the ADO67 was subjected to a rigorous programme of testing, including cold-weather analysis in Finland, during the brutal winter of early 1972. That spring, pre-production examples were even shown to journalists from *Autocar* magazine, intended to gauge the potential press reaction. By then, it was all-systems go and the new Austin was ready to be signed off for production. An extra £16 million of investment was poured into the Longbridge production plant, with 2,000 more workers recruited to boost output.

Stokes was certain of the Allegro's potential to win back sales, not only across the UK car market but on the continent, too. In an interview for the BBC, made at the new Austin's launch in 1973, he explained how:

> ... this covers the middle range between the 1100 and the 1750, where the bulk of the business is, and it's also a car which we think will appeal not only to the sophisticated British public, but to the sophisticated European public, which of course if very much greater now we're in the common market. It's a car we believe will appeal to European tastes as a whole.

With everything to prove, the car was given a name that summed up BL's optimism for its future. 'Allegro', a lively musical term, fitted the bill perfectly, sounding sufficiently cosmopolitan and – even more importantly – European. The ad copywriters got to work with lines such as 'timeless in durability... timeless in looks'. The Allegro was ready to be unveiled to the waiting world.

CHAPTER TWO

THE ALLEGRO SERIES I, 1973–75: NEW BEGINNINGS

On 17 May 1973, a selection of motoring journalists met in Marbella, Spain. The reason? This was the sunny venue for the new Austin Allegro's press launch, and there was a lot riding on this event going well. Examples from across the new car's sprawling twelve-model range were made available, to be put through their paces. And that's just what the journalists did.

British Leyland had learned their lesson from bad car launches. The Marina was a case in point. Only two years before, pre-production examples had been lent to the press, complete with worryingly under-developed front suspension. The hideous under-steer from the outclassed Morris Minor-derived components didn't go down well. Swift modification was called for from BL's engineers to

Allegro
The new driving force from Austin.

Moody, fog-filled publicity photographs gave the Allegro's launch a clear message: this is a serious car, for serious motoring – in theory, at least. BMIHT

reduce the problem, but by then it was too late – the Marina had started off on the wrong foot. That kind of bad publicity couldn't be allowed to happen again; there was too much riding on the replacement for the money-earning ADO16 range.

It was no accident that hot, dusty and rocky southern Spain had been chosen to showcase the Allegro. Allowing the press fleet to be thrashed over rough road surfaces was an ideal way for showing the flexibility of the new Hydragas suspension system, as well as BL's confidence in the new car. After all, if it could prove to be comfortable on the Mediterranean coastline, then imagine how well it would perform amidst the gentler terrain of the UK's urban areas.

This calculated risk looked to be paying off, with Alex Moulton's suspension coping well with the hard going. Gordon Wilkins of BBC TV's *Wheelbase* programme noted the improvement over the old Hydrolastic suspension, nick-named the 'shirt lifter' due to its ability to lift a gentleman's shirt out of the waistband of his trousers, through excessive pitching and wallowing. In the Allegro, no shirt was likely to become un-tucked.

The initial press reception was mixed regarding the car's styling, which was controversial from the very beginning. Some considered it to be neutral and balanced, while others regarded it as bloated and ugly. Still, the efforts that had been made to dress up the basic shape on the plushest versions,

To match its lively, playful name, the Allegro range was identified by pleasingly vibrant badging on the bonnet and boot-lid, with smaller, rectangular badges to denote the model. BMIHT

such as vinyl roofs, wheel trims and vivid colour schemes, helped to take the edge off these criticisms. However, it was too late to change anything now; BL would have to wait until the press reports were published. And so the twelve-strong Allegro model range was unveiled.

HOME ON THE RANGE

'We have tried with the Allegro to be all things to all men,' stated George Turnbull. With so much ground to cover, across the C-sector of the market, it was no accident that a dozen different variations on the new car were on offer. Its appeal would have to be even broader than that of the old 1100/1300. So, rather than merely offering two engine sizes, four were available. In addition, the two- or four-door saloon body styles could be specified in five varying standards of trim, depending upon the model. As a result, a dozen Allegro variants hit the streets in 1973.

At the bottom of the new Allegro range was the 1100 De Luxe. This was, as you would expect, a direct replacement for the outgoing Austin 1100, slotting into British Leyland's range just above the Mini Clubman. Available in two- and four-door saloon body styles, the emphasis was on economy

Simple, bright colours and minimalist exterior trim marked out the economy Allegros. These 1100 and 1300 A-series-powered saloons took over directly from the outgoing ADO16 range. BMIHT

A minimalist dream: flat, non-reclining seats, rubber floor mats and simple heat-pressed vinyl trim made up the cabin of the 1100 and 1300 Deluxe. At least the trim colours were cheerful. Note the simple door pull-handles. BMIHT

and value for money, despite the 'De Luxe' name tag connotations.

Externally, the body was simply adorned, in keeping with the model's bargain-basement image. A simple grille using horizontal bars, as well as front and rear 'Allegro' script badges, were scant decoration on the otherwise unadorned coachwork. Solid paintwork in a handful of colours completed this low-key appearance. Intriguingly, an exterior bonnet release was specified, as with the frugal Mini.

Within, the interior was a simple yet intriguingly exuberant place to be. Here, the Allegro's dashboard moulding could be found at its purest and least cluttered. Two dials were located in a small instrument binnacle: the first a speedometer and the second providing fuel level and engine temperature. Of course, the famous quartic steering wheel made its debut across the Allegro range, meaning that even the humble base model had this distinctive feature. Proudly embossed with the 'AUSTIN' name and the marque's coat of arms, it was certainly a talking point.

Elsewhere in the cabin, trimmings were simple. The non-reclining front seats and rear bench were clad in heat-pressed vinyl, matched by simple door-trims and bare metal door-tops. A simple pull-handle was fitted to each door, accompanying the plastic window-winder and flush-fitting door catches. Simple rubber matting covered the floor. Although undoubtedly minimalist, such standard fittings as a heated rear windscreen and two-speed wipers were not only useful, but also equipment that not all of its rivals could offer.

The old 1100 model's 1098cc A-series engine and four-speed, all-synchromesh gearbox were carried over for the Allegro, giving this new model the benefit of tried-and-tested mechanicals. An increase in weight put greater strain on the 49bhp unit, meaning that this was not a quick car, even if improved gearing gave the new model a marginal top speed advantage over the old ADO16 version.

However, the 1100 was an economy-oriented model, relying upon the engine's thrifty and tough characteristics, rather than out-and-out performance. As a result, the base-model Allegro was a sensible and relatively inexpensive option, retailing at £1,009.

The next rung up the Allegro ladder belonged to the 1300 De Luxe. This was identical to the 1100 De Luxe, save for the fitment of the 1275cc A-series engine. Again, this new Austin 1300 directly took the place of the ADO16 version that it had replaced. On the face of it, a difference of 177cc seemed hardly to be worth the addition of both 1100 and 1300 engines to the range. However, these two A-series engines had remarkably different characters.

The 1098cc unit was ideal, if ultimate fuel economy in urban areas was your goal. However, the 1275cc engine's shorter piston stroke and larger bore size made it freer-revving and slightly more powerful, making it a better compromise, if fast A-roads and motorways had to be tackled occasionally. As a result, the overall fuel economy of the 1100 and 1300 De Luxe both hovered around the 31mpg (9ltr/100km) mark.

Between them, these two models were intended to continue the sales battle over the hotly contested, small-saloon market sector. Conventionally engineered rivals, such as the Ford Escort 1100, Vauxhall Viva and Hillman Avenger, were being challenged by increasingly sophisticated foreign competition. The Peugeot 104 and Renault 5TL, as well as the Simca 1100 and Fiat 128, had moved the game on, in terms of comfort, road holding, practicality and value for money. With all of these cars also priced around the £1,000 mark, the smallest-engined Allegros had their work cut out.

SUPER HEROES

The further one looked into the Allegro range, the more features, gadgets and engines were available. Starting this off was the 1300 Super De Luxe. Mechanically identical to the poverty-spec 1300 De Luxe, the 'Super' title denoted a higher specification. Externally, a different, vertically slatted grille was joined by chrome-effect trim on the roof guttering, as well as a coach-line running along its flanks.

Inside, the interior had been made far more appealing than the more basic models. Plusher door-trims covered over the old-fashioned bare metal door-tops, as well as providing small padded arm-rests all round. The seats now reclined and there was carpet on the floors, while the dashboard was now adorned with a silver plastic trim strip across its middle, as well as a cigar lighter. The lucky 1300 Super De Luxe owner also had the benefit of an internal bonnet-release, keeping the battery and other engine bay components out of the reach of passers-by.

Interestingly, the front disc- and rear drum-brake set-up could be specified with a servo, effectively reducing the pedal pressure required. This was incorporated into the bulkhead-mounted master cylinder, replacing the existing item. As with the cheaper models, a push-button radio could be specified at extra cost.

Continuing the Super De Luxe theme was a 1500 version. This is where the range started to get really interesting; rather than taking over directly from an outgoing ADO16 model, the 1500 Super De Luxe was designed to carve its own niche in the 1.5-litre saloon market. Its capacious engine bay was filled by a 1485cc E-series engine, as previously seen in the Maxi. While the smaller A-series could be directly traced back to Austins from 1951, this single-overhead camshaft unit was a relative newcomer, and far more sophisticated. A single SU carburettor and modest state of tune marked this out as a car intended for general family motoring, however, with a reasonable power output of 72bhp.

Allegro 1100 & 1300 DeLuxe

From the outside, the base models featured horizontal grille slats and minimal decoration, although there was a choice of two or four doors. The 1300 Super Deluxe had a pinstripe and a flashier grille. BMIHT

To match the larger engine, a five-speed gearbox was fitted. In an age when even the smallest cars were expected to venture out on to the expanding UK motorway network, anything less than five gears – or at least four, with an overdriven top ratio – would have been unacceptable. The 1100 and 1300 Allegros may have been stuck in the slow lane, but the 1500 was intended to make light work of high-speed motoring. As a result, servo braking assistance was standard, with twin horns to blast lesser cars out of its way.

Visually, this altogether more impressive model could be identified by a hexagonal honeycomb-style grille, along with optional metallic paint. Within, the plain plastic facia had been given a lift, with mock wood trim set into the instrument panel,

while brushed nylon became part of the seat facings. All of this may seem like a riotous celebration of 1970s tastes, but the best was still yet to come.

SPECIAL TREATMENT

One more step up the range was the ultimate 1485cc-engined Allegro; the 1500 Special. It may have been Special by name, but British Leyland had clearly raided its big box of accessories. On top of the equipment for the 1500 Super De Luxe were a whole host of showroom-friendly goodies. A vinyl roof, stainless sill trims, wheel embellishers and reversing lights all jazzed up the four-door body shell. As was an option on all the new Allegro models, except for the poverty-spec 1100, a four-speed automatic transmission from Automotive Products was available, giving the option of clutch-free motoring.

Stepping across the aluminium sill kick plates revealed more mock wood trim than you could shake a stick at, with the tops of the doors, dashboard and even the centre of the steering wheel being adorned in the stuff. The central console may have been little more than a coin tray and clock mounted on the transmission tunnel, but this was heady stuff compared with the rubber mat-clad 1100 De Luxe. A glove box replaced the open passenger side-shelf, while eagle eyes would have noticed the vinyl gear lever gaiter and optional head-restraints. Even the boot had a courtesy lamp and carpet. However, the dashboard was still host

to merely a speedometer and combined temperature and fuel gauge.

For aspiring middle-class buyers, this Allegro appeared to be bang on the money, combining middle-range mechanicals with plenty of jewellery. Together with its Super De Luxe sibling, this 1.5 litre Allegro was aiming squarely at the territory occupied by the plusher Avenger, Escort and Viva models, in addition to more exotic European rivals, such as the Citroën GS and Renault 16. However, the Allegro hadn't finished its assault on the market yet.

Two pocket-rocket range-toppers combined the small-car body shell with a much more potent engine. By lengthening the stroke of the E-series engine to 1748cc, an extra 8bhp was released, to

The hardy A-series engine, in all its glory. The 1098cc was the best option for urban economy, but the stronger 1275cc made a better job of shifting the Allegro's bulk.

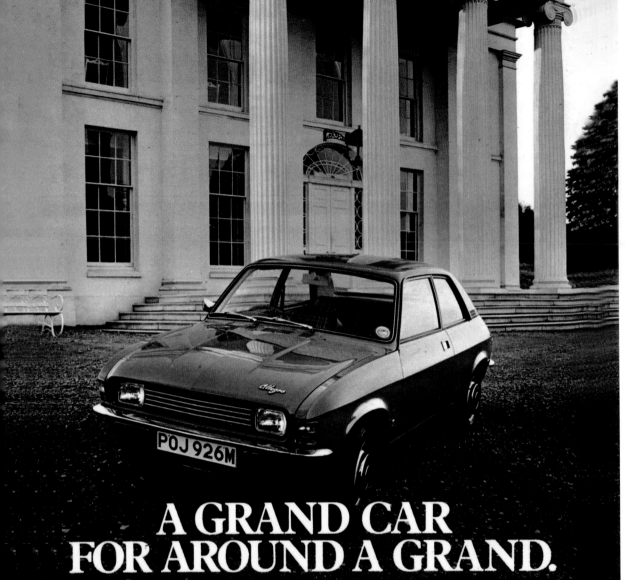

A GRAND CAR
FOR AROUND A GRAND.

The price of an Austin Allegro puts it in the economy class. You can buy the 1100 2-door De Luxe for just £1082.04.*

But a test run will quickly convince you that in some important respects, the Allegro gives as good as some cars costing twice the price. The ride and handling, for example.

The Allegro's Hydragas® suspension has a lot to do with this. No other car has Hydragas®.

Hydragas® is a unique system. It rides on gas. It absorbs dip and dive better, bumps better. Everything better. A jolt to our system won't jolt yours.

Hydragas® is a system that needs no regular maintenance. A comforting thought to go along with the comfortable ride. What's also comforting is the mileage. A touring mileage of 35.9mpg from the 1100 De Luxe. (Motor Magazine, 19.5.73.)

We've also done something special with our 'extras.' Most of them don't cost you extra at all.

The little touches like front disc brakes, underbody protection, wax injection of sill members, hazard warning lights, heated rear window, electric washers, 2-speed wipers, alternator, fresh-flow ventilation and what have you, all come as standard, and are included in the basic price.

All in all, you can't help agreeing what a grand car the Allegro is.

Until you remember there isn't just the 1100. There are 1300's, 1500's and 1750's.

Allegro isn't so much a grand car. It's more like the grand slam.

Austin Allegro
When you're travelling economy, go first class.

*RECOMMENDED PRICES FROM £1082.04 INC. CAR TAX & VAT.   DELIVERY CHARGES, SEAT BELTS & NUMBER PLATES EXTRA.

The smallest Allegros proved popular, due to their low cost, good economy and competitive equipment levels. Despite BL's hopes, these models out-shone the higher specification derivatives.
BMIHT

create the basis of the 1750 Sport and 1750 Sport Special.

SPORTING CHANCE

Intriguingly, the 1750 models were essentially upgraded versions of the 1500 Allegros. As a result, the 1750 Sport was identical to the 1500 Super De Luxe, but with the addition of the larger engine, special silver-over-black wheel-trims and a simulated-wood gear knob. Front seat head-restraints were now standard, while the instrument pod was widened to include a rev counter, as well as separate auxiliary gauges. The 1750 Sport Special had the same extra features but used the plusher 1500 Special as a starting point. A retail price of

£1,366.84, including VAT, marked out this range-topper.

So that was the range line-up. This was, in short, an Austin for a new age. The year of 1973 marked Britain's entry into the European Economic Community; the Allegro would have to compete in this common market. Its role was as a cosmopolitan new saloon, to take the fight for international sales to the door of its sophisticated European competitors, such as the Alfa Romeo Alfasud and Renault 16. Simultaneously, it would also have to offer a more intelligent choice to its low-tech UK rivals from the likes of Ford, Vauxhall and Hillman. It was, in the organization's own words, BL's 'song for Europe'.

It was clear that the Allegro had its work cut out for it. With hindsight, it's hard to argue that this was

A honeycomb grille marked out the upper echelons of the range, starting with the 1500 Super Deluxe. Vinyl roof coverings indicated success in 1970s Britain; the 1500 Special in the foreground was suitably attired. BMIHT

not the right direction for the company. Whether the Allegro truly was the design to carry BL forward though, winning over the hearts and wallets of motorists across Europe, was another matter.

HARD SHOULDER TO CRY ON

The same day as the official press launch, *Autocar* ran a series of articles on the new Austin. Intended as a promotional tie-in, much attention was given to its design and development, explaining its sophisticated suspension design, and what its makers intended it to offer to the average car buyer; a tried-and-tested method of product promotion.

In addition, *Autocar* published their road tests of two pre-production examples: a 1300 Super and a 1750 Sport Special. However, these effectively took some of the shine off this PR exercise; the two cars were not all that well received. In the weeks that followed, several more of the influential UK motoring journals published their own comparable road tests. The results were not good. Although some aspects of the design were praised, these plus points seemed to be far outweighed by its failings. General industry consensus was the same: despite high hopes, the Allegro didn't quite make the grade.

It wasn't all bad, though. The handling was deemed to be one of the Allegro's strongest features, in particular for the A-series engined models. The 1100 and 1300 versions were considered to be quite nicely balanced and safe-handling, albeit not quite in the same league as their lighter, crisper ADO16 predecessors. However, with over 100lb (45kg) of extra weight over the front wheels, and no changes to the suspension, the 1500 and

Initially, a single **SU** carburettor was the only option on the **E-series engines. This 1500** still offers plenty of spanner-wielding room in the spacious engine bay. Note the fitment of a brake servo.

Allegro 1500 Special

The true star of the 1.5-litre Allegros was the 1500 Special, rising above its poverty-spec siblings with its extra trim and interior clock. A vinyl roof, plus wheel and sill trims were clues. BMIHT

1750 E-series versions suffered from much more pronounced under-steer. Surprisingly, the smallest-engined Allegros were regarded as the nicest to drive spiritedly on twisting roads.

Praise was given to the Hydragas suspension, which was widely regarded as a significant step forward from the old Hydrolastic system. Its ability to maintain a smooth and level ride over rough ground was highly commendable, although a tendency to crash over potholes and the excessive body roll it induced during cornering were significant flies in the ointment.

Front-seat passenger accommodation was good, with comfy seats and a good driving position – another improvement after the old 1100's bus-like steering-wheel angle, as implemented by Issigonis. The levels of standard equipment certainly out-

did the Allegro's competitors. Also, the boot was larger than that of the old ADO16 design, even if it was accessed by an awkwardly short boot-opening; there was no hatch-back here. However, the rear-seat accommodation was let down by limited leg room and awkwardly shaped rear-door apertures, making access tricky. The sloping roof also ate away at the available head room, causing problems for taller passengers.

The basic A-series engined models were a bit noisy and not that sophisticated, but their commendable economy, despite the Allegro's greater weight over the 1100/1300, made up for this. On the whole, these basic models weren't at all bad. However, as the mountain that was the twelve-model range was scaled, expectations became higher and the criticisms became graver.

LEFT: **Compared to the 1100 Deluxe, the 1500 Special's interior was practically palatial. Part-cloth seat covers met woodgrain-effect plastic, although the second dashboard dial hole was still only occupied by a combined fuel and water temperature gauge.** BMIHT

BELOW: **Photographed in close formation, the 1750 Allegros were aimed at the gentleman who liked a bit of sporting performance from his family saloon. Ignore the ill-fitting driver's door and bonnet of the lead beige car; such production flaws were certainly not unheard of.** BMIHT

The performance of the range-topping 1750SS, which BL was so keen to promote as a true Q-car, proved a disappointment. Its torque steer under hard acceleration, coupled with an inability to top the magical 100mph (160km/h) barrier, weren't good. In all honesty, the big-engined Allegro's performance wasn't bad. However, there was only so much a long-stroke engine, breathing through a single carburettor, could do.

The strengths of rivals, such as the Renault 16TS, Fiat 124 Special, Hillman Hunter GLS and even Leyland's own Triumph Dolomite, only made things more difficult for the Sport and SS. *Autocar*, in their particularly merciless review, described the performance as the Sport Special as 'not particularly sporting or special'. Harsh words, but then there was indeed stiff competition in this category.

Although a prized feature on paper, the five-speed gearbox fitted to the E-series engine was quickly realized to be a flawed item. A vague, floppy gear-change, poor synchromesh and significant difficulty in engaging gears were all reported. One journalist's description of it being 'notchy at best, and infuriatingly obstructive at worst', was echoed by others. Sadly, significant drive-train harshness and considerable engine vibration through the bodywork were also reported.

QUARTIC IN A PINT POT

The initial reviews told a story of worthy improvements over the old 1100/1300 design, mixed with disappointing design flaws. Although not a bad economy saloon, its attempts to also be a lux-

That's better; *sans* number-plates and photographed in the orange desert glow, the 1750 Sport almost recaptures the sharpness of Harris Mann's original designs. Matt-black detailing extended to the lower half of the boot-lid, plus the distinctive wheel trims. BMIHT

OPPOSITE AND ABOVE: **A riot of colourful plastics and jaunty seat-covers, the interiors of the 1750 Sport and Sport Special were as kitsch as it got. Finally, a rev counter was fitted and two extra dials found their way into the enlarged instrument binnacle. Cheerful facias are finally coming back into fashion on today's cars.** BMIHT

urious, sporting mid-range contender, were clearly unsuccessful. However, on top of this was one feature that certainly didn't help the Allegro's image as a serious market contender: the quartic steering wheel. Although this quirky item is something of a 1970s style icon today, at the time it was seen by many as little more than a gimmick. Which, considering its last-minute inclusion in the car's design, it arguably was.

Motor described it as 'absurd' and a 'ridiculous device… it feels unpleasant and makes smooth driving around tight bends very difficult'. Many others, such as *Autocar*, agreed about this 'universally disliked' feature, with every road test of a new Allegro tainted by criticism of its steering wheel. However, while road testers found it hindered

spirited driving, BL management managed to make matters worse, by steadfastly disagreeing.

'It really is the technically correct shape for this particular car,' insisted Harry Webster, 'because the instruments are so positioned that you can view them straight through the steering wheel. It's a very comfortable wheel to hold.' Insisting that the road testers were wrong just added to the irritation. What's more, there was no denying that what was meant to be a novel sales' feature was rapidly turning into a bad publicity exercise. The British public quickly picked up on the absurdity of having a steering wheel with corners, and never forgot.

Interestingly, the Metropolitan Police force also rejected the quartic steering wheel on the grounds that it was impractical, when it placed an early order for 657 examples of the two-door 1100 De Luxe. Its special-order Panda cars, painted pale blue with white doors, were supplied with the round steering wheels fitted to other Austin and Morris models. Directly replacing the last of the ancient Morris Minor 1000 Panda cars, these new Austins proved to be just the ticket for patrolling duties.

TROUBLE AHEAD

The Allegro may have got off to a bad start, but things were about to get even worse. Criticism for its design had hurt the dynamic image of the 'new driving force from Austin', and its ability to compete was nothing like as great as BL had hoped. With these disadvantages, maintaining the 10 per cent market share, which the old 1100/1300 had once held, seemed dazzlingly optimistic, especially as that market was more competitive than ever. However, factors that extended beyond the drawing board would wreak the greatest damage on the fledgling Austin.

The year of 1973 was proving to be a particularly bad year for industrial strife, during an era that was plagued by poor relations with the trade unions across British industry. The previous year's coal miners' strikes and the resultant power cuts had ultimately led to the implementation of the three-day week, which was causing havoc with productivity. Disagreements between unions and management meant that strikes and stoppages were frequent across Britain's manufacturing base and, like the other large car-makers, BL certainly wasn't exempt.

Allegro 1750 Sport Special

Dark, jagged rock and the ghostly skeletons of dead trees can mean only one thing: it's the range-topping 1750 Sport Special. The SS was set apart by its vinyl roof and extra equipment. To cement its 'performance with luxury' identity, only the four-door body was available. BMIHT

Cracks were starting to show in the façade of the British Leyland Motor Corporation. Although attempts had been made to streamline the various entities that had all been thrown together by the merger, such as the reduction of manufacturing plants from seventy-four to fifty-nine, there was still a great deal of inefficiency and a huge workforce.

Further re-organization would have ensured a terrible backlash, prompting further strikes. Disruption to the supply chain of car components, both in their manufacture and transportation, made BL's output plummet. The first Allegros had been built at great difficulty, thanks to a strike at the Swindon body plant and production-line disagreements at Longbridge.

Then, in October 1973, the Arab–Israeli war brought about a colossal fuel crisis, driving prices up across the globe. A 50mph (80km/h) blanket speed-limit was introduced, in an effort to make petrol and diesel stocks stretch further. Thirsty cars had suddenly become too expensive to run, which was bad news for BL: it had just launched its fast, yet thirsty, MGB GT V8 and possessed a catalogue full of gas guzzlers, such as the Jaguar XJ12 and Triumph Stag. Its Australian branch had made the same mistake with the vast Leyland P76 saloon. The car market shrunk, and BL suffered. Only sales of the Mini increased, the old design enjoying a second youth.

Amidst such turmoil and chaos, quality control of these early Allegros was found wanting. Fit and finish varied wildly from car to car, with some being fine, others suffering from ill-fitting panels, water leaks and numerous mechanical teething problems. *Autocar* ran an early 1300 Super for 20,000 miles, experiencing collapse of the suspension, piston-ring problems, oil leaks, vibrations and a boot and interior that regularly filled up with water. These were all duly rectified by anxious BL agents, but such troubles did nothing for the car's image.

Making matters worse, insensitive garage maintenance was causing its own problems. Ignoring the correct jacking points and raising the car up from other, weaker points of its underside, resulted in body flex. Stories soon circulated in the press of rear windows falling out, although this urban legend was soon joined by a much more sinister claim. Over-tightening of the rear-wheel bearings was causing them to disintegrate and fail, leading to a series of crashes. This wasn't strictly the Allegro's fault, and warning stickers were quickly added. However, a BBC *Panorama* investigation into this problem did nothing to build public confidence in the Allegro.

From such a bleak and depressing start, it was clear that the Austin Allegro's problems were two-fold. First, its design clearly wasn't quite up to scratch, in light of fierce competition. Second, in service, it wasn't proving to be the reliable and well-built car that its buyers expected. As we shall see, neither of these significant issues would be insurmountable, but the damage had been done to the car's reputation during a breathtakingly short period. Still, things could only get better. As if to prove this, in mid-1974, an Allegro derivative appeared that was exactly what its target audience demanded. It's name? The Vanden Plas 1500.

KINGSBURY RULES

One of the most appealing Allegros to modern eyes is the 'posh' version of the Allegro. With ample helpings of wood, leather and good old-fashioned charm, the Vanden Plas 1500 certainly holds terrific classic appeal, even if its purpose is a little unclear. Why trim an Allegro to limousine standards? And why tack an old-fashioned grille on to its snout? Surely it's just a cynical marketing exercise? Well, no. The truth is that the VP was maintaining a tradition that had been long held by its ADO16 forebear.

The name Vanden Plas had been associated with coach-building since the days of horse-drawn carriages, but by 1962 it was securely attached to the luxury car division of the BMC empire. Fred Connolly, a big name in the supply of leather to the motor trade, approached Vanden Plas with an unusual request. The new Morris 1100 had recently appeared and he wanted the Kingsbury, London, firm to trim one to the same standards as its Austin-based limousines. It would, after all, be a great showcase for both Connolly's leather and Vanden Plas' exquisite craftsmanship.

The bespoke creation that was displayed to

This early Vanden Plas 1500 shows the model's unique frontal treatment in all its glory. Although slightly ill at ease with the car's styling, the protruding grille lends the car an almost vintage feel, an effect shared by the luxury interior trimmings.

From the rear, the upmarket effect was somewhat reduced, with only the badges and branded hubcaps suggesting that this was anything other than a run-of-the-mill Allegro. Note the rubber strip along the edge of the bumper blade.

the public was a true novelty, with luxury fittings squeezed into a small, thrifty, yet nimble family car. It caused quite a stir, with the unexpected result of numerous enquiries from potential buyers. BMC got wind of this and sensed an opportunity; so, at the October 1963 Earls Court Motor show, the production-friendly Vanden Plas Princess 1100 was unveiled.

Inside, Connolly leather trim was complemented by Wilton carpet, plus walnut veneer for the dashboard and door cappings. Folding picnic tables, typically found in mega-money machines, were fitted into the front-seat backs. MG 1100-specification mechanicals and a miniaturized version of the traditional Vanden Plas grille finished off the package. Although considerably more expensive than the basic Morris 1100, the Princess sold strongly.

Retired professionals, trading down from full-scale limousines, loved the car, as did more affluent families looking for a high-specification second or third car. From the very start, demand outstripped the supply. A 1967 engine upgrade to become the Princess 1300 only helped matters and over 40,000 examples were sold before it was discontinued in 1974, one of the last ADO16 variants to disappear. It was only natural that the new ADO67 range should provide a replacement for this final derivative.

NOSE JOB

Plans for a luxury Allegro were being made as far back as 1971. Roland Fox, the chief executive of Vanden Plas, was presented with an early prototype of the new Allegro. Spotting an opportunity, he made a sketch of the car's nose, complete with the addition of a traditional upright grille, in the style of the old Princess 1300. And so, once the – albeit disastrous – Allegro range launch was a thing of the past, it was time to reveal the new Vanden Plas 1500.

As its name suggested, this small, luxury saloon was based on the 1485cc E-series engined Allegro, available with a choice of the five-speed manual or four-speed automatic transmissions. The four-door Allegro body shell was used, complete with

Although only the smallest model in the Vanden Plas catalogue, the 1500 proudly displayed its coach-building heritage. Unlike its predecessor, the car was never badged as a 'Princess' and nor was it officially referred to as an Allegro, even though the shared 'genes' were clear to see.

Behind the round wheel of the VP 1500 (which never had the quartic item), the driver was treated to a walnut-veneer dashboard and door cappings. Seats were faced in Connolly leather, with front arm-rests and door storage-pockets. Instrumentation and switchgear was an intriguing mixture of standard BL rocker switches, black-faced Smiths' dials, plus a Jaguar-sourced warning light fitting. A rev-counter was never fitted; this was not a car built to be thrashed.

the very same chrome-adorned grille that Fox had envisaged. Wider and lower than the bolt-upright version used on the old 1300, it was accommodated on the 1500 by little more than a modified bonnet and front panel.

Even with the standard rectangular Allegro headlamps being carried over, the front end took on a remarkably 'antique' look. Hubcaps emblazoned with the 'VP' legend, elaborate chrome badging and slender black rubbing strips on the chrome bumpers completed the look. A passenger-door mirror and pin stripes were standard.

This was how the VP 1500s were delivered to the Vanden Plas works, minus interior trim. From here, the skilled trimmers got to work to give these cars their unique selling point. Thickly padded

seats were, predictably, trimmed in high-quality Connolly leather. With substantial arm-rests fitted to all door trims, and another fold-down rest between the front seats, these plush items could be transformed into mini arm-chairs. Rear passengers weren't neglected, with their own central arm rest.

Amidst the frenzy of deep-pile Wilton carpet, capacious door and seat pockets, and the cloth headlining, was an eye-catching walnut-veneer dashboard. Although using the same plastic lower mouldings as the standard Allegro, the wide, open shelf and instrument pod had been thrown away in favour of an attractive vertical panel. Black-faced dials flanked an elegant, coloured warning light cluster; an ex-Jaguar item, in fact. A proper glove box was provided, with additional under-dash shelving. Interestingly, Fox had insisted that the quartic steering wheel should by no means be used – another voice of reason on the subject.

These lavish trimmings gave the car a real sense of luxury. Interestingly, the car was never marketed as an addition to the Austin Allegro range, with the 'A' word neglected entirely in period adverts and brochures. However, nor was this new car a 'Princess', as the outgoing 1300 had been. This was a tactical move by BL's marketing executives, keen to distance the Vanden Plas brand away from the old BMC limousines it had long been associated with, and closer to the high-specification Jaguar models that had started to use the VP tag. This in turn freed up the 'Princess' name for the forthcoming Austin/Morris/Wolseley 1800/2200 replacement.

As a result, the 1500's identity within the BL range was a little blurred, being neither a true Austin nor a high-performance Jaguar-based cruiser. In fact, despite the VP's greater engine capacity and number of gears, performance was sluggish, particularly if the automatic gearbox was fitted. However, none of this was important. Retired, well-off gentlefolk took the 1500 to their hearts, ensuring steady sales throughout the otherwise turbulent 1970s. At last, this was an Allegro that was bang-on the money for its market niche, achieving small-scale success against the odds.

CHEAP AND CHEERFUL

Elsewhere in the Allegro range, things were a little less rosy. By 1974, the little Austin had managed to clamber up to fifth place in the UK top-selling charts, yet compared to the old 1100/1300's class-leading prowess this was still some way off BL's high expectations. Their initial decision to offer a dozen different models, in the confident style of Ford, suddenly looked unnecessarily excessive. So, the sprawling range was given a little pruning.

The two-door derivatives of several versions just weren't selling well, with the option of better rear-seat access from the four-door. So, this body style was deleted for the 1300 De Luxe, 1500 Super and 1750 Sport, leaving only the 1100 De Luxe and the 1300 Super De Luxe available with just two doors.

Incidentally, despite the Allegro's shaky start, the 1100 and 1300 versions were, at least, finding their feet. These cars' comfortable suspension, good

The luxuries continued into the back of the interior: the heavily padded and softly sprung rear-seat also featured a pull-down central arm-rest. Simple map-pockets were let into the backs of the front seats on early versions.

Vanden Plas 1500 production line at
Kingsbury, London.
Not to be published until 17 September 1974

British Leyland
Motor Corporation Limited
Public Relations
Photographic Services
Assembly Plant, Cowley, Oxford OX4 2LQ
Telephone 0865 777777 Ext. 234/5

This photograph may
be reproduced without
charge.
NEGATIVE
NUMBER
248407

The Vanden Plas works in Kingsbury, London, shortly before the launch of the 1500. 'Quality is our future' proclaims the proud banner. Curiously, quartic steering wheels are fitted to this early batch; VPs were only ever supplied with round items. BMIHT

equipment levels and commendable fuel economy, not to mention competent handling, ensured that they were competitive against the cheapest rear-wheel-drive Fords, Vauxhalls and Hillmans. A 10 per cent list price increase over the old 1100/1300 didn't seem to be able to blunt the usefulness of the basic Allegros.

However, the more expensive 1500 and 1750 versions, which Donald Stokes had confidently predicted to make up the bulk of Allegro sales, were competing in an entirely different market sector, and weren't doing anything like as well. This was perhaps a little ironic, given that the

main emphasis of the Allegro project had been to provide a wide range of engines and trim levels, branching out beyond its predecessors' 1100cc and 1300cc capacities. It was clear that the top end of the range needed to be spiced up, in an effort to kick-start sales. The answer came in the form of the Hi-Line.

HI AND MIGHTY

In September 1974, the 1750 Sport Special quietly disappeared, un-mourned and unnoticed. Its place was now occupied by a revised version, named the

Hi-Line to match the range-topping version of the Maxi. Externally, the addition of a double pinstripe and new badges meant that it looked almost identical to the old SS. However, significant changes had taken place beneath the bonnet.

Up until now, the 1750 models were only available with a single SU carburettor. The 76bhp produced as a result was severely disappointing for cars with 'Sport' in their names, as was their limited performance. All the while, however, the Austin Maxi Hi-Line had been using a twin-carburettor, higher compression version of this overhead camshaft engine, putting out a far healthier 90bhp. Transplanting this engine into the Allegro didn't require too great a leap of the imagination; finally, with the new HL, this had been achieved.

A double pinstripe and new badges were the limit of the external changes, but the performance boost was considerable. With a 100mph (160km/h) top speed, and dramatically improved top-end performance, the HL had gained much of the vigour that had been missing from the Sport Special. Of

The final Allegro body style, the three-door estate, was introduced in 1975. Its kick-up rear window line was reminiscent of the Reliant Scimitar GTE, yet this commodious new model was popular with scuba divers, as suggested here. BMIHT

course, with 78.5 per cent more power available than in the 1300 Allegro, with which it shared its underpinnings, this wasn't an out-and-out sports saloon. The engine's long-stroke design also meant it still wasn't on a par with comparable, yet sweeter-revving units, from German and Italian manufacturers. Yet, this simple mechanical upgrade was a welcome addition.

The 1750 Sport was also gifted with this improved powerplant. Although now only available with the heavier four-door body shell, this model was given a sporting new paint job. The matt-black boot-lid panel was retained but joined by prominent 'Sports' badges on the front wings and twin black stripes painted across the bottom edges of the doors.

COUNTRY ESTATE

There was a gap in the Allegro range, however. Ever since the end of the Second World War, Austin had always made a point of providing rugged and practical estate versions of many of its saloon car models. The last of these was the useful three-door 1300 Countryman. Following its demise in February 1974, and the disappearance of the larger 1.6-litre A60 Countryman a couple of years before, Austin was no longer represented in the medium-sized estate car sector, which accounted for 6.4 per cent of the overall UK market. It was the role of the final Allegro derivative to put this right.

Arriving in the summer of 1975, the Allegro estate took over from where the old Countryman

Although even more controversially styled than the saloon, the estate was arguably a very successful development of the original Allegro. The tail-gate lower panel lacked the ribs found on saloon boot-lids.

That large, top-hinged tail-gate dramatically improved on the pokey boot aperture of the saloon, creating a wide opening for all manner of loads. The standard rear valance, bumper and light units were retained. With the rear seat up, luggage accommodation was on a par with the Allegro's estate rivals. With the back seat dropped, load capacity was improved even further, making the estate the most versatile model of the range. Sadly, there was never a five-door variant.

models left off, offering two large passenger doors, a folding rear seat and a large, top-hinged tail-gate. Inside, a well-proportioned loading bay meant that this was a particularly practical model. Outside, the styling was undoubtedly even more controversial than that of the saloons, and certainly much more daring in its appearance.

Identical to the two-door saloon from the doors forwards, the rear flanks of the estate curved dramatically towards their rear, meeting in a spoiler-esque ridge across the rear of the roof. The rear side-window treatment had something of the Reli-

ant Scimitar GTE sports estate about it, while thick, rear pillars accommodated vents for the through-flow of air in the cabin. Today, such styling features are hardly unusual, but in 1975 they were criticized by the press. The Allegro just couldn't get it right.

Regardless of press reception, the Allegro estates were soon proving their worth as valuable multi-purpose cars. With only two versions on offer – the 1300 Super De Luxe and 1500 Super De Luxe – specifications matched those of the saloons. The estate was also a true hatchback, something which the other Allegro models were not. This hadn't been an issue in 1973. After all, that was the larger Maxi's job, offering a British alternative to such five-door offerings as Renault's 16 and the newly-launched Volkswagen Passat.

However, in 1974, the German firm launched its Golf, part of a new wave of compact hatchbacks. By the middle of the decade, Peugeot, Renault, Volkswagen and Ford, amongst others, all offered such designs. Both small and medium cars could clearly benefit from a large, rear hatch, and buyers knew it. As a result, the Allegro saloons were starting to look a little out-dated, with their small, conventional boot-lids. It wasn't alone in the BL stable; the Mini was also limited by its tiny boot, even if its other strengths kept it selling. Other European contemporaries who also made this mistake, such as the Alfa Romeo Alfasud, paid for this dearly until a hatchback could be added.

SUMMER BREEZE

BL had by now finished creating new and unusual Allegro derivatives but, shortly after the launch of the estate, an unexpected new version saw the light of day. Sold through dealer Spikins of Twickenham, was a convertible version of the Allegro, built by Crayford. This was no DIY job, though; Crayford had impeccable form for engineering roofless versions of popular saloon cars.

Based in Kent, Crayford had started building Mini convertibles, before moving on to conversions of Wolseley Hornets, Ford Cortinas, Corsairs and Capris, plus the Austin and MG 1100. Recently, they had even unveiled their conversion of the Morris Marina Coupé. All of these incorporated significant under-body strengthening, ensuring safety and rigidity, while some examples (such as the Ford Corsair) looked so good they could almost have been official manufacturer-built models. As the popular convertible car faded out of car makers' ranges during the 1960s, Crayford had worked to satisfy the demands of wind-in-the-hair motorists.

The deal was that, if the customer ordered a new Crayford Allegro through Spikins of Twickenham, the dealer supplied a brand new two-door Allegro to Crayford, who would in turn convert it.

This June 1975 photograph captures the excitement that accompanied the replacement of the unpopular quartic steering wheel with a round item. Probably. BMIHT

Sadly, the deletion of all two-door E-series Allegros meant that this could only be done with an 1100 or 1300, but some heralded this little rag-top as a replacement for the long-dead, but much-missed, Morris Minor convertible.

In the style of the old Minor, the standard side-window glass was fixed in place. However, floor-pan, sill and bulkhead strengthening negated the need for a T-bar to be fitted, giving its occupants unhindered access to fresh air. The vinyl-covered hood frame folded down to sit on the parcel shelf, although this did hinder rear vision somewhat. This conversion added an extra £480 on to the cost of the standard Allegro, meaning that an 1100 or 1300 Crayford had the capability to cost more than the latest 1750 Hi-Line. As a result, sales were limited. Still, for enjoyable summer motoring, such a car still scores highly indeed.

Technical Specifications:

Austin Allegro 1100 (1300) models, A-series engine, Series 1 & 2, 1973–79

Layout and chassis	Two-door/four-door saloon or two-door estate with all-steel unitary construction body

Engine

Type	BLMC 4-cylinder in-line
Block material	Cast iron
Head material	Cast iron
Cylinders	4-cylinder in-line
Cooling	Water
Bore and stroke	64.58 × 83.73mm/70.64 × 81.28mm
Capacity	1098cc/1275cc
Valves	Overhead valve, two valves per cylinder
Compression ratio	8.5:1/8.8:1
Carburettor	Single SU type HS4
Max. power (DIN)	49bhp@5,250rpm/54bhp@5,250rpm
Max. torque	59.6lb ft@2,450rpm/64.74lb ft@3,000rpm
Fuel capacity	10.5 gallons (47.7 litres)

Transmission

Gearbox	Four-speed manual, synchromesh on all forward gears (optional four-speed automatic for 1300 models)	
Clutch	Single dry plate, diaphragm spring type	
Ratios	1st	3.525:1
	2nd	2.218:1
	3rd	1.433:1
	4th	1.000:1
	Reverse	3.544:1
Final drive	4.33:1/3.938:1	

Suspension and steering

Front	Independent by unequal length suspension arms, trailing tie rods and by gas- and fluid-filled 'Hydragas' displacer units, interconnected front to rear
Rear	Independent by trailing arms and by gas- and fluid-filled 'Hydragas' displacer units, interconnected front to rear
Steering	Rack-and-pinion
Tyres	145-13 radial
Wheels	13in, pressed-steel disc, bolt-on
Rim width	4.5in

Brakes

Type	Servo-assisted hydraulic, front discs, rear drums with leading/trailing shoes
Size	9.68in discs front; 8in drums rear

Dimensions

Track

Front	53.62in (1,362mm)
Rear	53.70in (1,364mm)
Wheelbase	96.14in (2,442mm)
Overall length	151.67in (3,852.5mm) saloons
	155.22in (3,942.6mm) estate
Overall width	63.52in (1,613.4mm)
Overall height	55.04in (1,398mm) saloons
	55.80in (1,417.3mm) estate
Unladen weight	1,805lb (819kg) estate
	1,815lb (823kg) two-door
	1,847lb (838kg) four-door

Performance

Top speed	83.3mph (134km/h)/84mph (135km/h)
0–60mph	19.9sec/18.4sec

Technical Specifications

Austin Allegro 1500 & Vanden Plas 1500, Series 1 & 2, plus Allegro 3 single carburettor 1.5-litre models
(Allegro 3 twin-carburettor models), E-series engine, 1973–82

Layout and chassis	Four-door saloon or two-door estate with all-steel unitary construction body

Engine

Type	BLMC 4-cylinder in-line
Block material	Cast iron
Head material	Cast iron
Cylinders	4-cylinder in-line
Cooling	Water
Bore and stroke	76.2 × 81.28mm
Capacity	1485cc
Valves	Single overhead camshaft, two valves per cylinder
Compression ratio	9.0:1
Carburettor	Single SU type HS6/twin SU type HIF 4
Max. power (DIN)	68bhp@5,500rpm/77bhp@5,750rpm
Max. torque	79.5lb ft@3,250rpm/83lb ft@3,250rpm
Fuel capacity	10.5 gallons (47.7 litres)

Transmission

Gearbox	Five-speed manual, synchromesh on all forward gears (optional four-speed automatic with hydraulic torque converter coupling)
Clutch (manual)	Single dry plate, diaphragm spring type

Ratios (manual)		
	1st	3.202:1
	2nd	2.004:1
	3rd	1.372:1
	4th	1.000:1
	5th	0.869:1
	Reverse	3.467:1

Final drive (manual)	3.647:1

Ratios (automatic)		
	1st	2.612:1
	2nd	1.807:1
	3rd	1.446:1
	4th	1.000:1
	Reverse	3.467:1

Final drive (automatic)	3.8:1

Suspension and steering

Front	Independent by unequal length suspension arms, trailing tie rods and by gas- and fluid-filled 'Hydragas' displacer units, interconnected front to rear
Rear	Independent by trailing arms and by gas- and fluid-filled 'Hydragas' displacer units, interconnected front to rear
Steering	Rack-and-pinion
Tyres	155-13 radial/145-13 radial for 1500 Super
Wheels	13in, pressed-steel disc, bolt-on
Rim width	4.5in

Brakes

Type	Servo-assisted hydraulic, front discs, rear drums with leading/trailing shoes
Size	9.68in discs front; 8in drums rear

Dimensions

Track	
Front	53.62in (1,362mm)
Rear	53.70in (1,364mm)
Wheelbase	96.14in (2,442mm)
Overall length	151.67in (3,852.5mm) saloon
	155.22in (3,942.6mm) estate
Overall width	63.52in (1,613.4mm)
Overall height	55.04in (1,398mm) saloon
	55.80in (1,417.3mm) estate
Unladen weight	1,805lb (819kg) estate
	1,847lb (838kg) saloon

Performance

Top speed	91mph (146km/h)/100.2mph (161.2km/h)
0–60mph	16.7sec/12.9sec

CHAPTER THREE

THE ALLEGRO 2, 1975–79: GROWING PAINS

Having got off to something of a bad start, the Allegro had an awful lot of ground to regain in the sales race. British Leyland's hopes (not to mention a significant investment) were still riding on the car making up for lost time, and achieving something close to its original 5,000 cars per week production target. With the fate of these saloons and estates interwoven with that of the automotive conglomerate that depended on it, the Allegro simply had to do well.

The Allegro 2 colour schemes were as bold as ever; here, this Flamenco red estate is out-done by an even more vivid Blaze saloon at the back. Note the matching blue dashboard and seats for the four-door in the foreground... these were the 1970s, after all. BMIHT

Two-door, four-door and estate body styles continued to be offered, even if the range had been considerably pruned since the Allegro's 1973 launch. With the honeycomb grille now used across the whole range, it was difficult to distinguish between the different variants.

Unfortunately, the failings of the Series I were, by the end of 1974, well known. Serious development was needed, and fast, to rescue the model's credibility. Unfortunately, with precious little funding available to do so, BL had the unenviable task of improving the Allegro for as little outlay as possible. Sales' success would, in theory, generate enough cash for further improvement, but it looked unlikely that the car would achieve this without modification; it was a viscious circle. Under these troubled circumstances, the Allegro 2 phased out the Series I during October 1975.

In an effort to make the most cost-effective changes to the design, BL engineers had worked to rectify some of the car's most troubling characteristics. Rear passenger accommodation was a case in point. Although heralded in press releases as being greater than its 1100/1300 predecessor, the Allegro's rear quarters were still a little on the tight side, regardless of what the tape-measure said. A low, rear roofline, thickly padded seats and a narrow rear-door aperture for the four-door saloons all worked to make matters seem even worse.

Imaginative re-working of the inner body panels and rear-seat design was called for. By subtly reshaping the rear-seat squabs and shuffling the entire seat rearwards into the body shell, precious inches (almost five, to be precise) were freed up in the foot-wells behind the front seats. This modification may not have been immediately obvious, but it significantly improved the interior's space efficiency, coupled to greater front-seat adjustment. Sadly, little could be done about the low roof; even passengers of medium stature were still liable to bang their heads.

The excessive drive-train vibration came under scrutiny, too. The addition of two small hydraulic shock-absorbers incorporated into the engine

Although never the 'song for Europe' that BL had anticipated, the Allegro sold in moderate numbers in a number of European markets. This left-hand-drive 1300 estate originates from Sweden and is fitted with fog-lamps – something the British A-series models never got.

The old 'Allegro' script on the bonnet may have disappeared with the update but a new 'Austin' badge was fixed to the part-metal, part-plastic grille. Note the British Leyland roundel – this appeared on the boot-lid, too.

mounts, along with the mount medium being changed to conventional rubber, helped to further cushion the engine and transmission from the body. Additional drain holes in the boot floor, and drainage pipes from behind the roof pillar vents, went some way to reducing water leaks into the boot. Meanwhile, by adjusting the Hydragas springing rates to soften the front and harden the rear, the ride was dramatically improved. Of course, the quartic steering wheel had died earlier that year, and wouldn't return; round wheels were now the only option.

HONEYCOMB HIATUS

As worthwhile as these small improvements may have been, they were clearly not major revisions. Budget constraints meant that a face-lift was clearly out of the question, ensuring that the Allegro's dumpy looks would remain unchanged for the foreseeable future. However, a handful of cosmetic tweaks aimed to help the car on its way. The honeycomb grille was no longer exclusive to the range-topping versions, being employed throughout the range. In addition, black plastic sill covers and rear wheel-arch splash guards were fitted to all models; a simple move that lifted the appearance, and reduced the saloons' barrel-like side profile.

A range shake-up had also taken place. The bargain-basement model was, as before, the 1100 Deluxe. Mechanically unchanged and still with the option of both saloon body styles, this 1098cc economy stalwart had been treated to carpets in place of rubber mats, while the door trims were the same as the rest of the range; no more exposed steel on the door tops.

The thinly padded seats, which had previously been unique to this model, were finally replaced by the more comfortable items used in the other models. However, these had been cheapened and would not recline, while wipe-clean vinyl was the only choice of covering material. The Mini-esque external bonnet-release, unique to the cheapest Series 1 Allegros, was finally deleted, as were the silver facia inserts. A standard-fitment cigar lighter completed the picture. Not bad at all for the economy model, but there was plenty of scope for more creature comforts in the more expensive Allegros.

The 1100 was now the only 'Deluxe' model in the range, with the 1275cc variant now classed as the 1300 Super. The new estate body style was available alongside the two- and four-door Allegros, although this load-lugging variant featured a brake servo as standard (still an option for the saloons). Together with the four-door, automatic transmission was available for the estate.

Inside, the dashboard now had an unusual feature. Whereas the 1100 Deluxe still used the Series

LEFT: **Although badges were less flamboyant, the muted, square-cut script was accompanied by smaller, model-specific metal tags.**

BELOW: **Twin reversing lights were another feature that became standard fitment to all models, to suit changing regulations. To help keep up with the Joneses, twin boot-lid trim strips were fitted to any Allegro saloon of 'Super' designation or higher.**

1-style twin-dial instrument pod, all other models now featured a four-dial pod, with fuel and temperature gauges flanking two larger instrument holes. On the 1300 Super, these were filled with a speedometer and a blank space. Curiously, the latter was essentially a dial without any numbers or hands, being marked almost like a clock. Covered with the same clear plastic as the real instruments, the whole thing even lit up when the lights were on. This served as a constant and unavoidable reminder to the 1300 Super buyer that they hadn't bought the most Super Allegro.

Elsewhere, reversing lamps and a rear wash/wipe function for the estate were fitted as standard, while the reclining front-seats could be ordered with head-restraints as an optional extra. Metallic paint colours were also available at extra cost.

AUSTIN-TATIOUS

In the realm of the E-series engined-versions, the 1500 Super Deluxe had simply become the 1500 Super. From now on, the two-door saloon body would be the preserve of economy motorists and was only available with the A-series engine; this left the 1500 buyer with a choice of four-door or estate body styles. Velour seat-facings took the place of the old part-cloth trim, while rear-seat passengers were treated to a pull-down central arm rest. Aside from twin horns, this model was otherwise unchanged from its Series 1 predecessor.

The mid-range luxury model, the 1500 Special, also continued into the revised range, pitched firmly at the respectable suburban family buyer with its extra equipment. This model's crowning glory was undoubtedly its striking vinyl roof, accompanied by black-painted side-window frames and B-posts, as well as a matching black strip along the lower section of the boot-lid. Adding car-park kudos was the aim of these enhancements, but distancing this model from the poverty-spec A-series Allegros was always going to be a challenge.

Strangely, the blank dashboard dial was also a feature of both 1500 models, although the Special

Lower- to mid-range four-door saloons, such as this Blaze 1500 Super, represent the most numerous Allegro survivors today. Although lacking the luxury of a VP 1500, or the intrigue of an early Series 1, these bargain-basement models are still superb value everyday classics.

TOP: **The recently introduced estate body remained unchanged, with its vertically positioned vents in the rear pillars and funky curved side-glass. Note the rear wash-wipe function, serviced by a second washer-bottle and pump located within the spare-wheel well.**

BELOW: **Tough, wipe-clean vinyl was the order of the day for the 1300 estate interiors. These pint-sized wagons were expected to work hard for their living, as the old Austin 1300 Countryman had done. The cloth seat faces of the 1500 estates appeared almost decadent in comparison.** BMIHT

featured a clock, installed in a slender transmission tunnel-mounted central console. Why this clock didn't simply fill the blank in front of the driver is anyone's guess. An illumination lamp meant that owners could now see the standard-fitment boot carpet at night, had they desired, while head-restraints were also thrown in. Twin front fog-lamps and a passenger-door mirror were also part of the no-cost equipment. Unlike the Series 1 version, though, automatic transmission was available as an option.

Further range pruning had taken place at the top of the Allegro tree. The 1750 Sport was gone, leaving just the 1750 Hi-Line to carry across from the Series 1 top range line-up. As before, this represented the pinnacle of Allegro development, combining the highest equipment levels with the greatest performance.

Also in common with its Series 1 forerunner, the HL was the only model to fill that blank second dial aperture in the dashboard, with a tachometer taking its rightful place. Revised colour schemes, including metallic bright blue and bronze, were key

Although the 1100 Allegros kept the two-dial dashboard of the Series 1, a closer look at the 1300's four-dial dashboard reveals a bizarre feature: a blank dial. Astonishingly, this empty slot next to the speedometer even lit up with the other instruments. BMIHT

to the new model making the right visual statement. The sea of velour within was matched by a range of glorious 1970s paint shades, while brown and blue vinyl roof coverings broke the dominance of the previous all-black versions. It was a symphony of colour coordination. In common with the Vanden Plas 1500, the steering wheel was bound in leather.

Beneath the bonnet, the higher compression engine continued to be fed by a pair of SU HS6 carburettors. Instead of the usual vinyl coach-lines, slender waistline mouldings were attached, while, as before, the old SS wheel trims were re-used, with their colours reversed. As the sales literature rightly highlighted, this was the ultimate Allegro. 'Drive one soon' the ads people promised. 'You owe it to yourself.'

INNOCENTI UNTIL PROVEN GUILTY

As the British-market Allegros were given a re-

vamp, time was already being called on its long-lost Italian cousin: the Innocenti Regent. This fascinating offshoot of the original Allegro concept had only been in production for one season but, by 1975, it had reached the end of the road. Its creation followed a long relationship between its builder, Innocenti of Milan, and BMC/BL.

As far back as 1960, links between Longbridge and Milan were being forged, when scooter manufacturer Innocenti secured a deal to build Austin cars under licence. This was an important step for the Italian firm, aiding its progression from two-wheeled transport to four-wheeled passenger machines.

Its first offering had been an Italianized version of the Austin A40 Farina; appropriate considering the design's Pininfarina parentage. However, while the British Countryman estate made do with a split-folding tail-gate, the Innocenti version featured an innovative top-hinged, single-piece rear hatch. This cheeky little car's popularity showed Innocenti that it was on to a good thing.

A radio may only have been an option across the range, but a blank locating aperture and huge speaker grille dominated the centre of the dashboard. Simple long-wave and medium-wave sets like this were common, although an eight-track player, working through the single speaker, is still a joy to behold.

While the 1100 Deluxe buyers made do with relentless vinyl trim, the new owner of the 1300 Super was treated to cloth seats as standard, which also reclined. This quickly took on the appearance of an un-ironed shirt after relatively little use. Note the optional clock, which filled the blank dial space.

A vision of domestic harmony; BL's sights were still fixed on the middle classes with the Allegro brand. However, this was a hotly contested market, with fierce competition from both the UK and abroad. Plastic sill covers and splash panels were now universal fitment on all models. BMIHT

Very quickly, an attractive, locally styled version of the Austin-Healey Sprite was on offer, alongside Innocenti's Mini- and 1100-based models. Even an angular, Bertone-styled hatchback based on the Mini was offered, which would survive until 1993 with the addition of Japanese mechanicals.

However, by 1972, this independent company had been purchased by the ever-expanding BL. Now the British corporation had an Italian production facility to build localized versions of its latest cars. As the Allegro was BL's most European-friendly design, it made sense that an Italian-market version would be offered.

Named the Regent, the car that went on sale in 1974 in 1300, 1300L and 1500L guises, was very clearly an Allegro. However, there were a number

of unusual design details that were unique to this model. Aside from an all-black grille, boasting a single silver stripe and an off-set Innocenti badge, separate opening quarter-lights in the front door glass were the most obvious differences.

The higher-specification 'L' models weren't fitted with a vinyl roof, as the UK upper-range versions were. Instead, the whole roof was painted black, including the windscreen pillars and front scuttle panel. All models were fitted with side-indicator repeater lamps, mounted just ahead of the front wheel-arches. The wheels themselves, although steel, were significantly different from the British versions. Forlorn of hubcaps and wearing chromed wheel-nuts, the wheel centres were square, with ventilation slots around their edges.

Inside, the Regent was even more unusual. A unique version of the quartic steering wheel was to be found, but with a broad central panel and two angular alloy spokes. In fact, a round version of this wheel eventually found its way into the UK market Allegro Equipe of 1979. The Regent's dashboard was also unique to this model, with a significantly larger instrument pod. Only the four-door body shell was offered.

Sadly, this brave new model wasn't a match for the likes of the more appealing Alfa Romeo Alfasud, even though, like the UK Allegros, this too was plagued by build-quality issues. Sales of the Regent were disastrously poor, and as funds were already tight for BL the corporation decided to cut its losses. The corporation withdrew from Italy and retreated to more familiar markets. Innocenti was sold on to De Tomaso, surviving to see another day, but BL's fingers had been burnt by this rash venture.

CHANGING TIMES

Back in Britain, the Allegro was still having a hard time. Although not a vastly different car after its Allegro 2 revisions, due to the limit as to what could be achieved on such a tight budget, the select modifications had proved to be a step in the right direction. However, the competition hadn't stood still.

Up until now, the Allegro had possessed a distinct sales advantage over its British-made rivals, in

Externally, the 1500 Special resembled a 1750 HL, without actually being one. Aspiring owners could take comfort from the fact that, with only different badges and wheel trims, passers-by would have no way of knowing. BMIHT

Introduced in the final days of the Series 1, the 1750 HL took over from the old SS as the range-topping Allegro; note the new badging and the black strip across the lower boot-lid edge. Its sister model, the 1750 Sport, didn't survive into the Allegro 2 era. BMIHT

the economy class. The archaic rear-wheel-drive chassis was still common. The Ford Escort and Vauxhall Viva still used rear leaf-springs, as indeed did the Marina. Hillman's Avenger possessed more sophisticated underpinnings, but was still a front-engined, rear-wheel-drive saloon. It was a similar story with the competitors to the larger-engined Allegros, although the E-series engined cars' stumbling points meant that not even this could give the Austin an edge over the likes of the Hunter, Victor and Cortina.

However, the foreign competition had been hotting up. By the middle of the decade, Volkswagen was offering both the small Polo and, more worryingly, the Allegro-sized Golf. Both came in a wide range of engine sizes and specification levels, and together they launched an assault on the same market that the Austin was trying to succeed in. Let's not forget that the mould-breaking Golf GTi was just around the corner.

Renault, of course, had been a pioneer of the hatchback for a long time. The inexpensive, if

The latest version of the 1750 HL retained its twin SU carburettors. These, along with a compression ratio boost, gave the car a useful 90bhp. The automatic option was deleted; this would only be available on the 1300 and 1500 engines from now on.

slightly agricultural 4 was now backed up by the much more modern and cosmopolitan 5, as well as the bigger 16. A 12 saloon even provided for the more conservative buyer, who just wanted four doors and a separate boot. Elsewhere in France, Citroën's GS, although initially lacking the all-important hatchback, was on the right lines, as was the company's Visa.

Fiat's 128 was a nifty front-wheel-drive saloon, backed up by the supermini 127 and, despite its diminutive size, Simca's space-efficient 1100 had a useful hatchback. Alfa Romeo even had its tidy-handling Alfasud, although build-quality issues and the absence of a hatchback meant that, in some ways, it had much in common with the Allegro.

What's more, new Japanese offerings were quietly, but steadily, winning over British buyers, with their reliability, sound build-quality and good equipment levels. The frugal Datsun 120Y, as well as the more spacious 160B and 180B, demonstrated this perfectly. Foreign car sales were on their unstoppable climb from a mere 15 per cent of the market at the start of the 1970s to almost 50 per cent at the decade's end. BL management, and Donald Stokes in particular, didn't recognize this threat until it was much too late.

To make matters worse, Vauxhall was upping its game. In a bold move, the Luton firm launched its own small hatchback, to supplement the conventional Viva. Although still rear-wheel drive, the Chevette's compact three-door design made it a winner, becoming Britain's best-selling hatchback from 1975 to 1978. By this point, Ford had overtaken it with its front-wheel-drive Fiesta.

This was fast becoming an era of hatchbacks and superminis. Even the smallest new car was a versatile, multi-purpose machine, capable of screaming along motorways, squeezing through city centres

Recognize those wheel trims? That's right, they're the old SS items but with their colours reversed. Tinted glass was another 1750 HL-only feature, as was a laminated windscreen and the moulded trim along the car's flanks. Although not factory fitment, this example's full-length Webasto sun-roof is a desirable period feature.

or moving small bits of furniture, all while returning good fuel-economy. The only Allegro that could attempt to do all of this was the estate. However, in 1300 form its cruising ability was limited, while the 1500 lacked both the 1300's economy and the 1750's extra puff.

SECOND LIFE

These were changing times, and the game had moved on. Although a better car than the Series 1 had been, the Allegro 2 was still struggling to brush off its earlier reputation. Catch-up with the competition was proving tricky as a result. At its sales peak in 1975, 63,340 Allegros found new homes.

However, less than 2,500 cars were being built per week – only half the number that BL had originally envisaged – and this figure was decreasing rapidly. By 1978, the figure would be closer to 1,000. The new Trentham paint shop, which had originally been constructed at a cost of £1.5 million to deal with the Allegro's anticipated demand, was closed that year.

BL's problems as a whole were increasing. With many of its key money-earners struggling to sell, production disrupted by industrial action and a staggering number of employees, BL's money was bleeding away. State intervention was required to stop the organization folding and taking with it thousands of jobs. As a result, the National

 **Leyland Cars**   AUSTIN ALLEGRO
1750 HL 4 DOOR
NOT TO BE PUBLISHED UNTIL 14 OCT 1975

This photograph may be reproduced without charge.

NEGATIVE NUMBER
260407

This cheerful passenger is demonstrating the significant gains in leg room in the back of the Allegro 2. Criticized on the Series 1, clever panel re-shuffling made this second generation 1750 HL a spacious paradise of squashy velour. Note the head-rests. BMIHT

The Vanden Plas 1500 survived the 1975 range revisions largely unchanged, save for the general improvements in rear leg room. Plastic sill covers were now fitted, while the disc wheel trims were shared with the 1500 Special.

Enterprise Board took control in 1975, although BL was fast becoming a ticking political time-bomb. Cash for model development would become tighter than ever before.

However, things weren't entirely bleak for Austin. Harris Mann's second addition to the marque's range was unveiled to the world that year. Confusingly available with Austin, Morris and Wolseley badges, which flew in the face of BL's carefully planned marque identities, this was swiftly put right. Within months, the big new saloon was re-branded as the Princess, from Austin.

Its introduction in turn made the Allegro seem like a more harmonious part of the Austin range. The Princess' bold appearance, due to dramatic, wedge-shaped styling, made the Allegro look almost conservative by comparison. What's more, the continued use of Hydragas suspension and front-wheel drive for the new model showed faith in the Allegro's hardware. Of course, BL politics hadn't left the Princess alone; Mann's proposed hatchback was absent. As a result, the only option for buyers who wanted such a feature was the Maxi.

SPECIAL RELATIONSHIP

The larger-engined Allegros may have been struggling but the economy versions were finding much greater favour with the buying public. 'When you're travelling economy, go first class', a marketing strap-line used at the Series I's launch, did seem to count for something, it seemed. Although not

Although a curious concoction, the Vanden Plas continued to sell steadily in its niche market sector. Offering comfort and quality fittings in a small, economical package was what the 1500 did best. So much so, it very nearly survived into the 1980s.

quite as brilliant as their predecessors, the 1100 and 1300 model Allegros were accounting for the bulk of Allegro sales.

As a compact, economical and comfortable car, powered by the hardy A-series engine, the Allegro 2 seemed to be at its best. This was perhaps a little ironic, considering that the ADO67 project had been driven by a management insistence to offer more engine sizes than the previous 1100/1300 had done.

Meanwhile, the Vanden Plas 1500 continued to sell steadily in small numbers, largely untroubled by the turbulent affairs of the world. Retired gentlefolk still wanted their fix of wood and leather, after all. New wheel-trims, which sat beneath the hubcaps, were added to the car's list of standard equipment. As an added bonus, walnut picnic-tables finally found their way into the plush interior. These had been used on the previous 1300 Princess and folded out of the front seat-backs, each one even featuring a recess to safely locate a champagne glass. If the novelty factor of the VP 1500 had been great before, now it had gone through the roof.

On a lesser scale of luxury, the option of a clock was extended to the 1300 and 1500 Super models, now accommodated in the instrument pod's pointless blank dial space. This was undoubtedly a useful addition but, by 1978, the mid-range models still needed a sales boost. It was time for the launch of a special edition Allegro.

ABOVE AND BELOW: **Hurrah! The much-lamented loss of the VP Princess 1300's wooden picnic tables was finally put right. Mounted in the seat backs of the VP 1500, these walnut-veneered items featured delicate chrome handles, as well as an indent in which to rest your glass of bubbly. Very civilized.**

This line-up, seen at the Allegro's fortieth-anniversary bash at the Heritage Motor Centre in 2013, is headed by a Limited Edition model. Essentially a 1500 with all the trimmings, the LE could be ordered in Astral blue or Tara green, as here. Both were metallic, with contrasting side stripes.

Special editions were fast becoming the accepted way for car manufacturers to spice up an old model. The recipe was simple: raid the options' list for extra equipment, adorn the bodywork with bright paintwork and graphics, and add an exciting name. Citroën, for one, used this strategy extensively to aid sales of its old, yet still saleable, 2CV, throughout the 1970s and 1980s. It was time that Austin tried a similar tactic.

The result was the 1500 Special LE. 'For a limited period, the Allegro of a lifetime', the newspaper and magazine adverts cried. And they were right; in Allegro terms, this was a very highly specified vehicle. The bodywork could be ordered in the two metallic paint colours: the vibrant Tara Green

or the cool Astral Blue. Both were adorned with dramatic, multi-striped side graphics running the length of the car and colour coordinated to match the colour scheme.

Beige cloth seats, adorned with front headrests, dominated the insides, with their fabric boasting a striped pattern, similar to that used on the contemporary MG sports cars. A leather-bound steering wheel rim was standard equipment, as was additional sound-proofing. A tachometer took pride of place in the dashboard, while outside, fog-lamps and VP 1500-style wheel trims were standard, as was a passenger's door mirror. Beneath the bonnet, the 1500 E-series engine was fitted.

The individual requirements of export markets demanded ingenuity from BL's engineers. This Swedish Allegro is fitted with individual headlamp wipers, made from modified windscreen components. Steel guides stop the blades going astray during those fierce Scandinavian snow storms.

ENGLISH PATIENT

'The best reason for choosing our European car. It's British.' This marketing slogan from 1977 aimed to convince British buyers that the Allegro 2 was not only something to stir up national pride, but also belonged to the new breed of small European cars. BL certainly went to some lengths to back up this claim, offering the little Austin for sale in several European markets.

As 1979 dawned, a psychedelic new advertising campaign extolled the rapidly ageing Allegro's virtues as a roomy and lively family car. The meaning of the cryptic 'vroom vroom' tag line has been forgotten with the passing of time. BMIHT

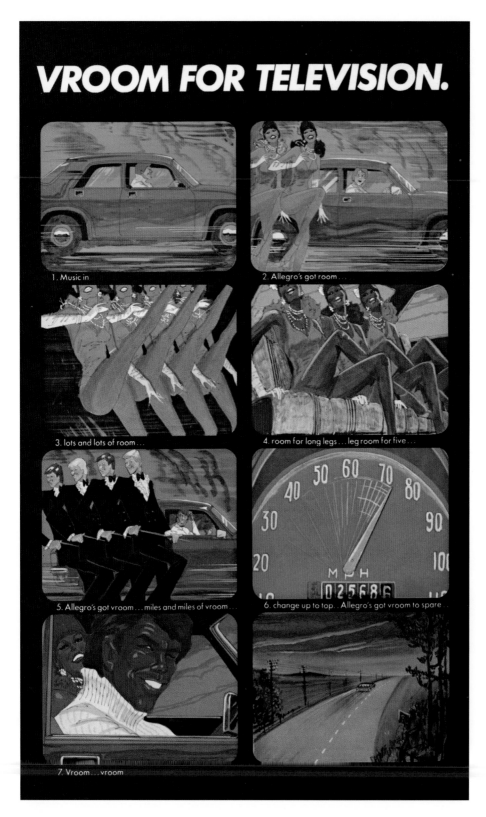

This storyboard guides us through the 'vroom vroom' campaign's prime-time TV advert. Essentially, man drives car, four long-legged female dancers join him in the car, man smiles. Four male dancers then parade past the car, man puts his foot down, car accelerates into the sunset. Only in the 1970s.
BMIHT

A dual-circuit brake system was introduced late in the Allegro 2's life, adding the modern failsafe system to the car's already decent stoppers. By this point, BL had decided that a brake servo was essential, not just a luxury for its upmarket models.

BL's Senneffe assembly plant in Belgium had started building Allegros from Completely Knocked Down (CKD) component kits during the dark days of the Series 1, with these cars then distributed across Western Europe. France had initially been a key target for the new Austin, taking the fight for sales on to the home soil of its Renault and Citroën rivals.

Billed as 'la grande Mini', the Allegro's role as a grown-up version of the cheeky little city car was clear. Television adverts showed sixteen people squeezing into the car's interior, in an effort to replicate similar stunts used to promote the Mini during the 1960s. This may have been a peculiar

tactic, but nevertheless, the car's Hydragas was a useful selling feature in a country used to soft, yet rugged, suspension systems.

Initially, a choice of '6CV' 1100, '7CV' 1300 and '8CV' 1500 engines was offered, all with the four-door body shell. Sadly, for patriotic French buyers, spoilt by home-grown designs, the Allegro wasn't quite the car for the job. By the time the Allegro 2 had arrived, a 1300 estate had joined the range.

In an effort to drum up sales, a special edition was conceived, unique to the French market. The 7CV Special was essentially the same as the UK market 1750 Hi-Line, but with a 1300 engine

Without doubt, one of the most glorious yet peculiar **BL** cars of all time, was the Allegro Equipe. Aiming to breathe a bit of excitement into the strangely shaped Austin, its silver paintwork with Starsky and Hutch-esque graphics was eye-catching to say the least. Sports clothing was evidently required to drive one. BMIHT

beneath its bonnet. As a result, this economy special was loaded to the hilt with goodies, such as velour interior trim, a rev counter, Hi-Line wheeltrims, a passenger-door mirror and a vinyl roof, amongst other features.

There were other quirks unique to European-market Allegros. In Sweden, the harsh winter weather had prompted the development of such special features as headlamp wipers, while Belgian and Dutch models utilized four round headlamps. These wouldn't be seen on British Allegros until the advent of the Allegro 3.

After the unsuccessful Innocenti Regent project had ended in late 1975, BL returned to the Italian market during the spring of the following year, offering conventional Austin-branded Allegros. These were available as the 1100 De Luxe, in two- or four-door guises, and the 1300 Super, available either as a four-door saloon or as an estate.

On the other side of the globe, New Zealand was also being introduced to the Allegro. BMC had long had good relations with the local car-building industry, with models such as the Morris Minor light commercial vehicles being built there, long after their UK counterparts had ceased production. The New Zealand Motor Corporation started assembling Allegros from CKD kits in 1975, just months before the Allegro 2 arrived.

Initially, only the 1300 A-series engine and manual gearbox were offered. Mirroring British tastes, the 1500 – which was only offered with an automatic transmission – proved to be significantly less popular and was swiftly deleted. After the NZMC took on contracts from Honda in 1976, assembling the Civic and Accord, the writing was on the wall for the Austin; slimming down the range of Allegro colours to sober browns and blues was a sad indication that the car's days were numbered. The last Allegro was built in the antipodes in 1980.

EQUIPE ON RUNNING

Back in Britain, the Allegro's development would take yet another unexpected twist. There was no denying that the little Austin was clearly built for comfort, rather than speed. Following the demise of the 1750 Sport, the only version with even vaguely

Those vivid orange and red stripes were stickers, extending along the flanks of the car and up the roof pillars. Not since the death of the 1750 Sport had the two-door body been available with the 1750 engine.

sporting pretensions was the 1750 HL. However, even that wasn't an out-and-out road-burner. An equipment-heavy specification, plus only a choice of the heavier four-door body shell, meant that its reasonable performance was blunted by weight. This car was aimed at the more conservative buyer, who valued plush trimmings above road-burning performance.

Meanwhile, BL's marketing department longed for a more exciting Allegro model to promote, which would in turn sprinkle a little excitement on the rest of what had become a rather unexciting range. Something was needed that would generate a little showroom traffic, pulling punters in through

This is Allegro as you have never seen it before.

The Equipe.

It looks like it moves and moves like its looks.

The powerful 1750 transverse overhead cam power unit has twin carbs and five forward gears and develops 90 bhp at 5,500 rev/min.

Which simply means 0-60 mph in 10 secs.

And a top speed of 100 mph.

Sports car performance in anybody's language.

Standard features include alloy road wheels, low profile Michelin 165/70 – 13 radials, halogen headlights, front and rear foglamps, tinted glass,

metallic paintwork and a matt black front spoiler designed to maintain stability at higher speeds.

And that's only the outside.

The interior features alloy spoke steering wheel, tachometer, clock, push-button radio, inertia-reel front seat belts and unique cloth seating in racing check.

See the Equipe at your nearest Austin Morris showroom.

But you'd better be quick because the Equipe is a Limited Edition that's going to move like its looks.

Vroom, vroom.

Allegro Equipe /// from Austin Morris with Supercover.

NOW EVEN VROOMIER

Unique alloy wheels and low-profile tyres, along with numerous cosmetic tweaks, tried desperately to sweep away the Allegro's stuffy image. As the 'vroomier' buzz words suggested, performance was particularly lively, if still not quite on a par with its sportiest rivals. Today, the Equipe is a sought-after collector's item. BMIHT

the doors of BL dealerships and subsequently generating sales for the cheaper models. After all, this was a strategy that Ford had been successfully employing for years.

Normally, such a plea would have fallen upon deaf ears. Develop a new, sporting version of a middle-aged design, which was only experiencing moderate success as an inexpensive family car? Madness, it would have been regarded as. However, in a startling move, BL announced a brand-new addition to the Allegro family during the spring of 1979. On paper, it answered the prayers of those long-suffering advert copy writers.

Radical was the best way to describe the new arrival's appearance. The re-use of the standard Allegro two-door body was clear to see, but the way this 'shell had been employed was startling. Metallic silver paint was laid across its panels, with

vivid red, orange and black stripes draped across the side flanks. Starting at the front indicators, these bold stick-on graphics made their way along the length of the car, before curving upwards and running across the rear roof pillars.

In contrast to these bright hues, the valances, plus the lower portions of the body sides, were painted matt-black. A matt-black grille was adorned only with a red stripe and solitary Austin badge, while the standard bumpers had also been stripped of their usual chrome. What's more, the previous 'lip' spoiler of the Allegro 2 was gone, in favour of a larger, full-width black plastic air-dam, spanning the width of the front valance. A set of attractive GKN alloy wheels completed the external visual make-over.

If this confrontational exterior suggested that BL had gone barking mad, then the interior only

The Equipe's interior was similarly riotous in its design. A modified version of the Italian-built Innocenti Regent steering wheel was fitted, along with tartan trim. These Bay City Rollers-esque seat-covers were similar to those used in the Triumph TR7, another Harris Mann design.

The shape of things to come? These two immaculate Equipes demonstrate this model's true legacy: its plastic front spoiler, which became the basis of the Allegro 3 face-lift, later in 1979. For quirky retro fun, the Equipe is unbeatable.

British Leyland's plant in Seneffe, Belgium, handled the production of many of the higher specification Allegros towards the end of the 1970s. These, and many Minis, were then shipped back to the UK. Interestingly, quad headlamps were fitted to many of the cars it built there for mainland European markets, which would later appear on the UK Allegro 3. BMIHT

added to this impression. Specified in black, the usual plastic trim had been joined by jaunty tartan-covered seats. The result was akin to sitting on a Bay City Roller; but then, what else would you expect from a car with Starsky and Hutch-style side stripes? The icing on the cake came in the form of a smart, alloy-spoked steering wheel. This had in fact started life in the equally unusual Innocenti Regent, but its square rim had been swapped for a more conventionally shaped version.

This wasn't merely an exercise in off-the-wall styling modifications, however. Beneath the bonnet lay the same twin-carburettor 1750 engine as used in the HL, putting out a healthy 90bhp, while the rest of its underpinnings were all standard Allegro parts. Setting this Austin aside from the rest of the BL stable was its name, emblazoned across the nearside bonnet corner and lower B-panels. By using the French word 'Equipe', the new Allegro's title conjured up visions of motor racing and sporting prowess.

The whole exercise was a brave attempt to help the Allegro appeal to a much younger and trendier audience, shaking off the design's frumpy image. For sheer courage alone, BL should be applauded for producing what would be one of its most memo-

rable and unashamedly outrageous cars. What's more, the plan to drum up a bit of publicity with the Allegro Equipe proved to be successful.

Nobody was fooled into thinking that this was a first-class sporting machine, on a par with the likes of the ultra-sharp Volkswagen Golf GTi or the powerful Talbot Sunbeam Ti. Priced at £4,360 after tax, it was almost as expensive as Renault's formidable 5 Gordini. However, its entertaining performance, thanks to a useful 103lb ft of torque from that large-capacity, long-stroke engine, in addition to the bouncy standard-specification Hydragas, only added to the fun factor.

Not even the fact that the Equipe was ultimately no faster than the 1750 HL, nor a tendency for its tyres to go flat, courtesy of the special alloy wheels, could detract from the car's novelty value.

The Equipe's production run was limited to 2,700 examples, but these attention-grabbing cars were certainly effective in ushering prospective Austin buyers into BL showrooms. During the summer of 1979 the Allegro experienced a small surge in sales, thanks in no small part to the attention grabbed by the range's silver flagship model. However, the Allegro's final incarnation was just around the corner.

Technical Specifications

Austin Allegro 1750 models, plus Allegro 3 1.7-litre single-carburettor models and Vanden Plas 1.7, E-series engine, 1973–82

Layout and chassis	Four-door saloon with all-steel unitary construction body

Engine

Type	BLMC 4-cylinder in-line
Block material	Cast iron
Head material	Cast iron
Cylinders	4-cylinder in-line
Cooling	Water
Bore and stroke	76.2 × 95.76mm
Capacity	1748cc
Valves	Single overhead camshaft, two valves per cylinder
Compression ratio	8.75:1
Carburettor	Single SU type HS6
Max. power (DIN)	76bhp@5,000rpm
Max. torque	97lb ft@2,300rpm
Fuel capacity	10.5 gallons (47.7 litres)

Transmission

Gearbox	Five-speed manual, synchromesh on all forward gears (optional four-speed automatic with hydraulic torque converter coupling)	
Clutch (manual)	Single dry plate, diaphragm spring type	
Ratios (manual)	1st	3.202:1
	2nd	2.004:1
	3rd	1.372:1
	4th	1.000:1
	5th	0.869:1
	Reverse	3.467:1
Final drive (manual)	3.647:1	
Ratios (automatic)	1st	2.612:1
	2nd	1.807:1
	3rd	1.446:1
	4th	1.000:1
	Reverse	3.467:1
Final drive (automatic)	3.8:1	

Suspension and steering

Front	Independent by unequal length suspension arms, trailing tie rods and by gas- and fluid-filled 'Hydragas' displacer units, interconnected front to rear
Rear	Independent by trailing arms and by gas- and fluid-filled 'Hydragas' displacer units, interconnected front to rear
Steering	Rack-and-pinion
Tyres	155-13 radial
Wheels	13in, pressed-steel disc, bolt-on
Rim width	4.5in

Brakes

Type	Servo-assisted hydraulic, front discs, rear drums with leading/trailing shoes
Size	9.68in discs front; 8in drums rear

Dimensions

Track	
Front	53.62in (1,362mm)
Rear	53.70in (1,364mm)
Wheelbase	96.14in (2,442mm)
Overall length	151.67in (3,852.5mm)
Overall width	63.52in (1,613.4mm)
Overall height	55.04in (1,398mm)
Unladen weight	1976lb (896kg)

Performance

Top speed	97.8mph (157.4km/h)
0–60mph	12.7sec

Technical Specifications

Austin Allegro Equipe, plus Allegro 1750 and 1.7-litre twin-carburettor models, 1974–82

Layout and chassis	Four-door saloon with all-steel unitary construction body

Engine

Type	BLMC 4-cylinder in-line
Block material	Cast iron
Head material	Cast iron
Cylinders	4-cylinder in-line
Cooling	Water
Bore and stroke	76.2 × 95.76mm
Capacity	1748cc
Valves	Single overhead camshaft, two valves per cylinder
Compression ratio	9.5:1
Carburettor	Twin SU type HS6
Max. power (DIN)	90bhp@5,500rpm
Max. torque	103lb ft@3,100rpm
Fuel capacity	10.5 gallons (47.7 litres)

Transmission

Gearbox	Five-speed manual, synchromesh on all forward gears	
Clutch	Single dry plate, diaphragm spring type	
Ratios	1st	3.202:1
	2nd	2.004:1
	3rd	1.372:1
	4th	1.000:1
	5th	0.869:1
	Reverse	3.467:1
Final drive	3.647:1	

Suspension and steering

Front   Independent by unequal length suspension arms, trailing tie rods and by gas- and fluid-filled 'Hydragas' displacer units, interconnected front to rear

Rear   Independent by trailing arms and by gas- and fluid-filled 'Hydragas' displacer units, interconnected front to rear

Steering   Rack-and-pinion

Tyres   155-13 radial

Wheels   13in, pressed-steel disc, bolt-on

Rim width   4.5in

Brakes

Type   Servo-assisted hydraulic, front discs, rear drums with leading/trailing shoes

Size   9.68in discs front; 8in drums rear

Dimensions

Track

  Front   53.62in (1,362mm)

  Rear   53.70in (1,364mm)

Wheelbase   96.14in (2,442mm)

Overall length   151.67in (3,852.5mm)

Overall width   63.52in (1,613.4mm)

Overall height   55.04in (1,398mm)

Unladen weight   1,976lb (896kg)

Performance

Top speed   104mph (167km/h)

0–60mph   11.0sec

CHAPTER FOUR

THE ALLEGRO 3, 1979–82: TWILIGHT YEARS

During its second incarnation the Allegro had started to mature. Design details had been tweaked and build-quality issues attended to, with the result that it was starting to become the car that it should have been from the start: functional, reliable and comfortable. Sales were still lagging behind British Leyland's original, wildly optimistic targets but, despite the tarnished reputation, by the mid- to late-1970s acceptable numbers of new Allegros were finding homes. There was even a summertime flurry of sales during 1979, thanks in part to the curious 'vroom vroom' advertising campaign.

However, the world hadn't stood still, and the Allegro's design had dated swiftly following its

A new look for the old Allegro and a new catchphrase to help market it. 'Supervroom' may have been a cynical advancement on 'vroom vroom' and 'vroomier,' but this banner heralded some big improvements. This was the quad-headlamp 1.7HL, now at the head of the new range. BMIHT

launch. Although reasonably successful in its 1100 and 1300 guises, the rest of the Allegro range had failed to carve much of a niche in their respective market sectors. Rivals were becoming faster, roomier, more economical and better looking.

Hatchbacks were becoming the norm, rather than the exception, and restricting this feature to the three doors-only estate meant that the Austin was lagging behind. With the 1980s appearing on the horizon, Austin Morris needed an all-new design to re-assert its lost footing on the small- to medium-sized family car battlefield.

The trouble was, the cash-strapped and government-owned BL was in no fit state to launch such a marketplace assault. Wheels were in motion developing both small- and medium-sized cars that would be able to fight the good fight in this brave new world; these would become the Metro and the Maestro.

Unlike the brochure-only designation 'Allegro 2,' the whole range was now badged as the 'Allegro 3'. Models were now recognized in litres, rather than ccs, representing a move from the 1950s method of naming cars. As a result, the old 1300 engine was now re-branded '1.3'.

As the new Austin Morris logo found its way onto many **BL** designs, the 'plughole of doom' roundel made one last appearance on the Allegro's boot-lid. Later Allegro 3s used cut-out plastic lettering, with the corporation's new logo taking precedence.

However, both were still in development and neither was yet ready to be launched. There was no option left to Austin Morris but to update the Allegro, bolstering the old-before-its-time design for one last attempt at sales success. The result would, arguably, prove to be the Allegro's finest hour.

BACK IN BLACK

In September 1979 the existing Allegro range was swept away and in its place was launched the new Allegro 3. 'Supervroom' was the new car's catch-phrase, following on from the 'vroom vroom' advertising campaign of early 1979. Cynics quickly dismissed this as a face-lift to breathe life into a rapidly ageing design, and it's easy to understand

Déjà vu tainted the new face-lift, with the Equipe's plastic front spoiler now used universally. The battering ram-esque bumpers were, in fact, hollow. Plastic end caps and an all-new plain grille completed the front end's new look.

The rear bumper followed suit, complemented by larger, squarer rear light clusters. These now incorporated the reversing lamps. The number-plate was raised up to sit on the re-shaped boot-lid, with a regulations-friendly rear fog-lamp mounted beneath the bumper.

why. Heavier bumpers, external plastic trim and revised interiors did little to disguise the familiar body shell, while the choice of 1100, 1300, 1500 and 1750 engines was the same as before. However, there was much more to this new car than met the eye.

For starters, fuel economy inched upwards across the range. While this was welcome on the larger-engined models, for the 1098cc and 1275cc versions, which were marketed on thrift, this was a huge bonus. Official British Leyland figures recorded that, driven at a constant 56mph (90km/h), the latest 1300 manual Allegros could top 46mpg (6ltr/100km), over 5mpg more than the outgoing Series 2 versions. Astonishingly, thanks for this new

economy drive could be directed at the now-dead Allegro Equipe.

The limited-edition Allegro Equipe had been a brief yet remarkable phenomenon, taking the Series 2 design to a conclusion that nobody had anticipated. With a predictably short shelf-life, its racy alloy wheels and Starsky and Hutch-style bodywork graphics had swiftly disappeared forever. However, the model's black plastic spoiler would live on, fitted to every Allegro 3 model built.

The original intention of the Equipe's under-bumper spoiler may have been for visual effect as much as anything, cleaning up the fussy valance and screwed-on steel 'lip' trim, but it actually did a good job of improving aerodynamics. The bold claims of Allegro 3 literature really were correct when describing 'a front spoiler that enhances roadholding and, through a more efficient air-flow, fuel economy'. The result was a 10 per cent improvement of the drag co-efficient, from 0.44 to 0.4, which in turn boosted fuel economy across the range by a remarkable 11 per cent. The small-engined Allegros, in particular, were now thriftier than ever before.

While the Equipe had worn black-painted versions of the original thin blade bumpers, the Allegro 3 was equipped with much larger, square-section replacements. This was the greatest cosmetic difference from earlier models. By this point, the industry had been moving away from slender chrome fenders for some years. Approaches varied from the internally strengthened rubber-faced battering rams of contemporary Volvos, to simpler, easily changed plastic panels, as with the Renault 5. Even Leyland's own MGB and Midget had adopted substantial rubber bumpers to meet US regulations. The overall effect was the same though; chrome was out and black was in.

Save for mounting brackets, the Allegro's square pressed-steel bumpers were completely empty, while the end caps were moulded from hard, non-absorbent plastic. The new black fenders may have looked like a nod to ever-changing safety standards, but in fact they were no more sophisticated than the simple items they replaced.

The rest of the bodywork changes were somewhat limited. Saloon boot-lids lost their ribbed-effect panel in place of flat steelwork, which in turn now located the rear number-plate. This was

Allegro 1500 Special

Seen those quad headlamps before! Many Belgium-built Allegros, such as this French market 1500 Special, had been using this lighting arrangement several years before it was adopted for the UK market cars. BMIHT

Larger, black plastic door mirrors were shared with the latest Mini, while front indicator repeaters were introduced. Tacking such parts on to the old design was only a quick-fix solution to keep the Allegro saleable; a replacement for the 1980s was being hastily developed.

illuminated by two rectangular lamps mounted on the bumper. The tail lamps, which on the previous models had been curved to match the rear corners of the bodywork, were now much squarer in profile. These new lamps not only jutted out further, but also incorporated a pair of reversing lamps. Now, a single, rear fog-lamp was located beneath the rear bumper.

Despite the new rear lamps, the front indicator and side-lamp units remained unchanged, even if they were now joined by round wing-mounted indicator repeaters. Most of the Allegro range was still fitted with rectangular headlamps and halogen bulbs. However, in an effort to set the higher specification models apart from the lesser equipped versions, four round headlamps were fitted. Both lamp arrangements were now set into black plastic slatted grilles, replacing the familiar honeycomb grille. A new design of black, plastic-covered door mirrors was fitted, still with a blanking plate, unless a passenger mirror was specified.

Intriguingly, the Allegro was now devoid of a grille badge. In fact, there was scarcely any identification on the car. The 'Allegro' legend may have once been proudly displayed, but now the car's name and parentage was restricted to two boot-lid badges, either side of the rear number-plate. The left-hand badge simply said 'Austin' alongside the BL roundel, while 'Allegro 3' and the model designation – 1.3L, for example – was printed on its partner. These low-key badges hardly shouted of Austin Morris' pride in the updated model.

Body-wise, the talk of wax-injected sills and bitumastically coated undersides continued as before, although there were very real bulkhead sound-proofing upgrades introduced with the new model. On a long journey, in particular, these could make the world of difference, and made the 3 a slightly more civilized driving machine.

What's more, three new colours were now available in the otherwise familiar paintwork charts. Champagne, which was essentially a metallic beige, and yellow were nothing out of the ordinary. However, the third shade, Applejack green, was quite remarkable for its vivid neon hue. Although a peculiar and ultimately unpopular choice for a car aimed at the more conservative buyer, Allegros painted in this colour were amongst the most visually challenging ever built.

The overall effect of the styling revisions was a neutral-looking car; not pretty but not ugly either. Initially, the cheapest Allegro was the 1.1L, but when its 1098cc engine was swapped for the 998cc A-Plus unit, it simply became known as the 'L'. BMIHT

Anticipating future regulations, the new Allegro's dashboard made use of the new universal warning light symbols, stacked in the centre of the new instrument pod. The bargain-basement L, with its hard-plastic steering wheel, had vertical fuel and temperature gauges in place of the missing tachometer; an old trick. BMIHT

INSIDE JOB

From the outside, the Allegro 3 make-over was hardly extensive. Inside, it was a different story. Numerous revisions, although small, combined to transform the appearance and feel of the interior. The most striking feature was a new dashboard. Gone were the brightly coloured, hard plastic dashboards of the Allegro 2, in favour of a black, impact-absorbent item.

This new facia followed the same principle as before, with an instrument pod set atop a wide, open shelf, designed to carry assorted knick-knacks. However, this shelf was deeper, with a removable rubber mat, to stop items rolling away. Gone were the slender air-vents of the past, in favour of larger, multi-directional vents – a real improvement in heating and ventilation. A larger, removable ashtray was also hidden by a sliding plastic panel in the centre of the dash top.

A larger, more rounded instrument pod featured a deeper hood to reduce glare, while a single sheet of Perspex covered black-faced instruments. Although these varied from model to model, all now shared the same pod, regardless of their contents. Universal European control and warning light symbols were now used, stacked between the instruments at the centre of the pod. On base models, the speedometer was flanked by a combined fuel-level and water-temperature gauge; these functions were split between two smaller dials on higher specification models, making way for either a clock or tachometer.

If the Allegro 3's facia predicted the new Metro of 1980, then this was no coincidence. Austin's small-car interior-design philosophy had favoured simple designs and open storage shelves since the A30 of the 1950s. The heating and ventilation controls were now simpler and chunkier, making them less fiddly to use. A rotating fan-control button operated the two-speed blower motor, while a simple, single, temperature-control slider replaced the previous two, with a second slider to control the direction of the air flow.

However, the same old lower dashboard mouldings soldiered on, available only in black. A central radio-speaker continued to live behind its moulded grille, and hazard warning lights, rear-screen heating controls and cigarette lighter were all as before. However, the driver's side cubby-shelf was restricted by a bank of plastic switches – or blank switch locators, in lesser models – while the radio

A re-worked dashboard top included larger, multi-directional air-vents in place of the old 'letterbox' version: a small detail that made all the difference in summer.

Here's a familiar sight. The lower dashboard moulding, with its antiquated single speaker grill, was carried over, while the old Radiomobile push-button radio continued as an official Unipart accessory. However, this new turn-screw heater-fan switch was popping up across the Austin and Morris ranges.

blanking panel was now a separate removable panel, rather than having to be cut or drilled out to fit the radio as before.

Continuing the revision of the controls, the column stalks were rounded off, being joined on the steering column cowling by a shaped rocker switch. This controlled the lights, replacing the previous facia-mounted item. The choke control was in turn re-located to a plastic panel on the left-hand side of the steering column.

Most notably, however, the standard issue BL two-spoke steering wheel was gone. Now, a new 'corporate' design was in use, similar in appearance to the four-spoke shape already seen on later MGBs. This new wheel would soon be utilized on

the new Metro of 1980. Its lowered spokes were claimed to be more beneficial for driver comfort, and in practice they certainly offered a more ergonomically sound location for the driver's hands on a long drive.

In the centre was a removable steering-column nut cover, which was again devoid of any badging. The Leyland roundel and 'Austin' coat of arms in this position were now mere memories. Eerily, there were no reminders at all from behind the wheel of the mighty BL empire. However, the existing flat-topped gear levers remained unchanged, as did the transmissions they were attached to.

The combined effect of these small changes was enough to give the rapidly ageing design a slightly

Reclining seats were still out of reach for the L/1.1L owner, although tough fabric seat faces were a welcome change after the Allegro 2's use of vinyl. Interior door catches had been redesigned, although the back seat did without a central arm-rest; a frivolous luxury. BMIHT

more modern feel. It was hardly going to make the Allegro feel like an entirely new car, but it was a cost-effective way of helping to keep the little car up-to-date and stop it going stale, if hardly at the white heat of technology. By improving on the existing design with tweaks and amendments, the driver was the one who benefited.

Elsewhere in the cabin, there were few changes. The chrome buckle-type door-release handles made way for hard-plastic levers, while the window-winder handles lost their shiny silver handle centres. New, more rounded door-rests were now fitted. The seats were the same as before but treated to yet another new stitching pattern for their covers.

MODEL BEHAVIOUR

With the Allegro range in general having been given a spruce-up, it was seen fit to shake up the model designations. Initially, from September 1979, the simple tags of 1100, 1300, 1500 and 1700 were used – dispensing with recognition of the 1750 power-

plant's extra 50cc – but within three months, these all disappeared, as did any suggestions of 'super' or 'deluxe', which were terms very much rooted in the 1960s. As another sign of changing times, a more contemporary model range – and more in line with the likes of Ford or Vauxhall – appeared.

At the bottom of the tree sat the 1.1, still using the same venerable old 1098cc version of the A-series engine that had first seen the light of day in the Morris 1100 of 1962. A slight step up was the 1.3, again with the slightly more urgent 1275cc A-series as before. These two were the most basic Allegros, aimed firmly at the economy motorist looking for reasonable comfort and refinement but at a bargain price. As such, their specifications were suitably pared-down.

Nylon facings for the non-reclining seats and a twin-dial dashboard, consisting of only a speedometer and combined fuel and temperature gauge, were accompanied by a basic hard-plastic version of the new four-spoke steering wheel. Only a driver's door-mirror was fitted as standard (the passenger mounting holes being blanked off) and

This magnificent sight is an early 1.3L, showing off the plastic wheel-trims that came in with the 1979 face-lift (as well as the Maxi 2). Reminiscent of alloy wheels, these were fitted to the 1.3L and upwards; lesser versions had to make do with the old chrome hubcaps.

1980 was the last year that the trusty A-series was offered, in 1100 and 1300 guises. Painted in black, these were ousted in favour of the Metro's re-worked A-Plus units, which were painted red. Internally beefed up, with a different carburettor and exhaust, the new 1.3 version was significantly more powerful. Even the 1.0 lump's performance was on a par with the old 1100.

While old favourites survived in the colour charts, such as **Russet brown**, a particularly vivid hue shocked the conservative Allegro buyers. **Applejack green**, shared with the jaunty new Metro, still divides opinion to this day. Love it or loathe it, few Allegros are as eye-catching.

the outgoing Allegro 2's chrome hubcaps were still clinging on with these models. The 1.1 was available with either the two-door or four-door body shells, but no estate as before, or an automatic option. The 1.3 could be ordered as an automatic or an estate (lacking load-bay carpet, incidentally), but there was only a four-door saloon option.

The next rung of the ladder was occupied by the 1.3L. The L may have had 'luxury' connotations but the improvements over the basic 1.1 and 1.3 were limited. For starters, the 1.3L could be ordered as a two-door saloon (unlike the basic 1.3), as well as a four-door and with the three-door estate shell. There was the same four-speed manual gearbox or automatic as an extra-cost option. Outside, an exuberant double coach line was laid across the flanks, while the body-coloured window frames and B-pillars of the lesser Allegros were now painted black.

The front seats were reclining, a locking glove-box lid was fitted, the fuel filler cap now had a lock, the rear seat had a central arm-rest, a clock was fitted (and the fuel and temperature gauges split) and a cigar lighter made an appearance. The steering wheel was, for this model, made of a softer, springier feeling plastic, with a larger central boss cover. The 1.3L also introduced the Allegro 3's new wheel-trims. Made of silver plastic, they covered the entire wheel save for the wheel nuts, which the trims actually sat beneath. Individual plastic nut-covers were then fitted.

The 1500 and 1750 engine sizes reappeared in the 1.5L and 1.7L. These both shared the same trim level and equipment specifications as the 1.3L, and were both available as either a four-door saloon or an estate. Interestingly, the 1485cc E-series engine of the 1.5L was now equipped with twin SU carburettors and a twin down-pipe exhaust, but was only available with the five-speed manual gearbox. The 1.7L, on the other hand, was only available as an automatic, using a single-carb version of the 1748cc powerplant (as was the tradition for automatic versions of BMC/BL front-wheel-drive cars). Range rationalization had deemed that the 1.5L should be more sporting and friskier in feel than the 1.7L, which was in turn more relaxed.

HL HELL

Now the model range started to get really interesting. At the top of the tree were the HL models.

Constant suspension amendments ensured that the Hydragas didn't pitch and roll like a yacht in a swell. In fact, the last Allegros were the best to drive, meaning that this little 1.3 estate had a lot going for it. Roomy, frugal and comfortable, only the lack of a fifth gear was a concern in the speed-obsessed 1980s. BMIHT

Spaciousness was still a strong selling point for the estate. Aside from the dashboard, the interior trim had changed little. Eventually, redesigned front seats and dark 1980s fabrics would stamp out such warm browns and beiges. BMIHT

Marking these elite Allegros out from the rest of the pack were a number of visual differences. Only available with the four-door body shell, these cars were trimmed with a black vinyl roof, as well as the aforementioned quad headlamps. The twin, under-bumper mounted fog-lamps made a re-appearance, again mounted in place of the cosmetic grille vents. Those big black bumpers now had silver inserts, along with a centre line, extending across the plastic bumper end-caps, while a matching side rubbing stripe in silver and black was fitted.

At last, a passenger-door mirror was now standard fitment, as was a smattering of little extras. A push-button LW/MW radio, a tachometer, front head-restraints and velour seat-facings, an intermittent windscreen-wiping function and a central floor-mounted console, with a clock and change tray, were all added to the spec sheet, along with a vinyl cover for the spare wheel. The speaker grille in the centre of the dashboard was now empty; amplification was entrusted to a pair of stereo speakers, mounted on the A-panel trims in the front foot wells. Meanwhile, an all-new central console was fitted, incorporating a square clock. This was luxury, Allegro 3-style.

Intriguingly, the HL's engine and transmission options weren't as you might expect. Up until now, the mechanical specification had dictated the level of trim within. That was no longer the case. Alongside the anticipated 1.7HL was a 1.5HL, taking over from the old 1500 Special. What's more, a 1.3HL was also available, combining the plushest Allegro features with what had proved to be the most popular engine capacity.

The 1.3HL and 1.5HL were mechanically identical to their lesser siblings. However, the 1.7HL could be ordered as a manual or an automatic. The automatic 1.7HL was a single-carburettor model; essentially, just a 1.7L with an improved specification. The 1.7HL manual, however, was now the new range-topper, using the five-speed gearbox with twin carbs for better performance.

Much was made of this in Allegro 3 sales' literature: 90bhp, a 100mph (160km/h) top speed and a

As the older estates had done, the Allegro 3 load-luggers used as many parts from the saloons as possible, from doors to tail lamps. The black-painted B-pillars and window surrounds were particularly effective in making the estate look longer and more modern. BMIHT

0–60mph time of 11sec, all compared favourably with the much wilder looking, and now discontinued, Allegro Equipe. Sadly, the days of the Allegros being showered with publicity, both good and bad, were long gone; the range re-vamp went largely unnoticed by the automotive world.

By now, Longbridge was gearing up for production of the new Metro, due to start the following year. As a result, the most lavish, well-equipped Allegros, in addition to many Mini models, were being assembled at BL's Senneffe plant instead, before being brought back into the UK.

Curiously, the Allegro 3 front spoiler managed to sneak its way on to a number of V-registered Allegro 2s, such as this estate, not to mention a handful of W-registered Vanden Plas models. A big-bumpered VP 1.5/1.7 prototype was built, but never put into production.

HI-FIVE

With their order placed for a new Allegro 3, the eager Austin customer could peruse the display of official accessories in the corner of the showroom. In truth, personalization using manufacturer-supplied parts had been an option with BL cars long before the Allegro arrived. Since 1964, BMC Special Tuning had been offering performance parts to private individuals, which had been developed by the Competitions Department for use in their race and rally cars. This was, after all, a golden era of DIY tuning and modification.

Even after the BMC Competitions Department was closed, and the BL era got underway, the re-branded Leyland Special Tuning continued to offer a range of performance-enhancing modifications for the keen motorist with go-faster intentions. More serious carburettors, manifolds, exhausts, cylinder heads, camshafts and more were available, alongside spot lamps, rally seats and steering wheels. The Stage One engine-tuning kit could even be fitted without invalidating the car's warranty. For those with money to burn, the performance – or indeed, appearance – of any Austin Morris car could be improved. The Allegro certainly wasn't left out.

Leyland Special Tuning finally closed its doors in 1980. Even at this stage, however, a selection of official upgrades was being offered for the Allegro. Austin Morris knew that this Austin was hardly the preserve of wannabe racing drivers, so the 'Studio' range of additions was divided into three categories, each allowing owners to personalize their cars to

varying degrees. 'Touring' accessories, such as fog-lamps and medical kits were joined by 'Rally' parts. These included pod-mounted tachometers, external rally-style spot-lamps and even the Equipe-style steering wheel.

However, the most fascinating category of Allegro additions belonged in the 'Hi-Style' category.

It may have been on its last legs, but BL was still marketing accessories for the Allegro as late as 1979. The keen owner could personalize their 1.3L with 'Allegro' branded body graphics, a vinyl roof, an Equipe-style steering wheel or even a Unipart-branded medical kit. Those were the days. BMIHT

The Vanden Plas derivative didn't escaped modification before its demise at the end of 1979. In the name of cost-cutting, the 1500 (renamed the 1.5) was given twin carburettors and was only available with a manual gearbox. A 1.7 version was available but only in single carburettor, automatic transmission form.

These dealer-fit options were intended to add a bit of spice to any Allegro's exterior. A lowly 1.1, for example, could be adorned with a vinyl roof, a garish exhaust tail-pipe finisher and even neon-coloured graphics for the side flanks, which proudly included the 'Allegro' legend. BL may have long since lost its pride in the Allegro, but at least these modifications echoed a little of the flamboyance and colour of the car that had appeared in 1973.

VANDEN PLUS

Up to now, the Vanden Plas 1500 derivative had continued to sell steadily to a small band of loyal followers. Its unique selling point had centred on its high-quality fittings and old-world charm, albeit .... As a result, there was very little that the Allegro 3 range re-vamp could do for it, without damaging its raison d'être.

Black plastic fittings would have cheapened this coach-trimmed curiosity.

However, the 1500 wasn't left completely alone. Austin Morris had tried to adorn it with the new spoiler and bumpers, but these experiments were deemed unsuccessful. However, for 1979 and 1980 other changes were made. The flat-panelled boot-lid had deleted the earlier version across the range, so was used on the VP, albeit unadorned; the number-plate was still located beneath the rear bumper. The earlier arrangement of curved rear light units and separate reversing lights was retained, but with the addition of a plastic rear fog-lamp. Black wing-mirrors and windscreen-wiper arms were further additions, but that is as far as it went. Externally, the VP had largely escaped ....

Inside, the front seats were now, at long last, equipped with the head-rests that had been missing

VANDEN PLAS

The Vanden Plas 1500, and later 1.5 and 1.7 versions, may have been curious creations, but they continued a tradition of coach-building that could trace its roots back as far as the end of the nineteenth century.

Carrosserie Vanden Plas was founded in Belgium by Guillaume van den Plas with his three sons. An English subsidiary of this coach-building firm emerged in 1913 but, when the firm collapsed in 1923, the name and rights were acquired by employee Edwin Fox and his brothers, to become Vanden Plas (1923) Ltd. The firm moved from Hendon to a factory in Kingsbury, north-west London.

Their speciality was hand-built coach-work and trimming, with bodies being built on chassis for exclusive machines, such as Bentley, Alvis, Daimler, Rolls-Royce and Delage. From the late 1930s to the end of the war, Vanden Plas worked closely with De Haviland in the manufacture of aeroplanes. However, by 1946, Leonard Lord had bought the company for £900,000, with the purpose of building the bodies for Austin's new chassis and 6-cylinder engine. Thus, Vanden Plas became a subsidiary of Austin.

The A120 and A135 used Vanden Plas' own bodies, coupled to Austin underpinnings. However, the Austin A105 Vanden Plas of 1958 started the trend for having readily assembled Austins trimmed by Vanden Plas at Kingsbury. This practice would continue for the next two decades. Due to popular demand, the A105 was followed by the new Princess 3-Litre of 1959. Although based on the Austin Westminster, this was badged exclusively as a Vanden Plas. The addition of a Rolls-Royce developed engine created the legendary Vanden Plas 4-Litre 'R.'

The 1100 Princess was a novel concept for the company, combining upmarket trimmings with the mass-market Morris 1100. However, the model proved so popular it eventually developed into the Princess 1300 in 1967, before surviving well into the British Leyland era. Its 1975 Allegro-based replacement, the Vanden Plas 1500, was similarly successful in its niche market.

By 1972, top versions of the V12-powered Daimler Double-Six were being trimmed at Kingsbury. However, by now, changes were occurring. Having been associated with the everyman Austin brand for so long, British Leyland wanted instead to attach this luxury marque with its more exclusive Jaguar–Daimler division. As the 1970s progressed, models such as the Double-Six and prestigious DS420 limousine accounted for over 60 per cent of Vanden Plas's turnover.

Following the 1.5 and 1.7 models' demise (as the 1500 had become), and the closure of the Kingsbury works in 1979 due to cost-cutting, Vanden Plas became a brand attached to plusher versions of BL cars. The Rover SD1, Austin Ambassador, Maestro, Montego and Metro were amongst those that appeared wearing those familiar badges. Fittingly, this identity was last used on a version of the Rover 75, before Vanden Plas becoming little more than an unused name in Nanjing Automobile Group's portfolio of British marques.

The saloon never looked quite as sleek as the face-lifted estate, due to its dumpier styling. This 1.5 HL features the later, rectangular, indicator side repeaters; the higher spec 1.5 HLS was identified by quad headlamps and silver inserts in its bumpers.

THE A-SERIES ENGINE

Although merely a compact, small capacity 'four', the unassuming A-series engine can quite rightly claim to be one of the most successful British engines of all time. This unit's long life started in 1951, beneath the bonnet of the new Austin A30. This inexpensive four-seater saloon was launched as a spiritual successor to the marque's original people's car, the Seven. As part of its up-to-the-minute specification, a scaled-down version of the 1200cc A40 engine was fitted. Producing a mere 28bhp from 803cc, this early A-series was no ball of fire. However, its efficient combustion chamber design and overhead valve layout, in an era of ageing side-valve designs, showed potential.

BMC was quick to exploit this. Within five years, a much-improved 948cc unit was fitted to the new A35 and Morris Minor 1000. With a greater capacity and much more robust bottom-end, the A-series was transformed into a sweet-revving delight. Engine-tuning firms, such as Speedwell and Downton, were quick to improve upon its 37bhp power output, with the 1958 Austin-Healey 'Frogeye' Sprite doing likewise.

Well-proven as an economical and remarkably tough engine, the A-series was chosen for Issigonis' Mini. Down-sized to 848cc, it was turned 90 degrees to sit transversely across the width of the car. The gearbox was located within the engine's sump to save space; ground-breaking for 1959. The Morris 1100 of 1962 stretched both the Mini's basic concept and its engine. This 1098cc long-stroke unit's strengths were its torque and easy fuel economy, ensuring its adoption for the cheapest Allegros.

Mini Cooper development saw a frenzy of development, spawning 970cc, 997cc, 998cc and 1071cc versions. The 1964 Cooper 'S' 1275cc engine inspired the creation of a mainstream, economy-minded version in 1967. Starting life in the 1300 range, as well as the Sprite and MG Midget, this A-series was the best all-rounder. With a wider bore yet shorter stroke than the 1098cc unit, it could not only rev harder, but was more powerful and less stressed.

The Allegro inherited the 1275cc engine from its forerunner, which also propelled the heavier Marina. Tight funds and British Leyland internal politics meant that the A-series would become the powerplant of choice for the new Metro of 1980, prompting one last development push. Improved and strengthened to become the A-Plus, the engine range was rationalized to just 998cc and 1275cc capacities. With the demise of the old 1100 engine, a 1-litre version of the Allegro was now offered.

The MG Metro Turbo extracted a staggering 93bhp through forced induction, becoming the most powerful production version of the A-series/A-Plus line. However, times were changing, and the little engine was falling behind the increasingly efficient designs from competitors. The fact that the transverse versions were saddled with a four-speed gearbox was a significant shortcoming in an era when even city cars were expected to cope with motorway miles.

for so long on this luxury model, although the rest of the interior remained unchanged. It was under the bonnet where the most significant difference could be found. Alongside the 1500 version – now re-named the Vanden Plas 1.5 – a new 1.7 model could be ordered. In reality, these two cars were mechanically identical to the Allegro HL models.

Instead of the previous manual and automatic options on the original single-carburettor 1485cc E-series engine, the former was now only available as a manual. Automatic buyers had to opt for the 1.7, which used the 1748cc E-series. Using only a single carburettor, there were no illusions that the 1.7 was a sportier drive than the 1.5; instead, its torquey, more relaxed nature made it better suited to the automatic transmission.

There may have been another Vanden Plas model to choose from, but by now the writing was on the wall for this historic brand. In an effort to cut costs, British Leyland opted to close the Kingsbury factory, which had been home to the marque for almost six decades, in November 1979.

Trimming and finishing of the last 1.5 and 1.7 models was passed to MG's Abingdon plant, taking advantage of spare production capacity. However, with the dawning of the new decade, the little Vanden Plas models became entangled in BL politics. This factory too was closed in October 1980,

Intriguingly, the 1.3 Maestro and Montego mated the A-Plus with a five-speed Volkswagen gearbox, necessitating the unit to be rotated by 180 degrees. An enterprising solution, no doubt, but moving increasingly large cars was a lot to ask of the old engine. Its siamesed exhaust ports and ageing push-rod design very much belonged to the past.

The new K-series twin-cam engine powered the Metro from 1990, leaving the A-Plus to soldier on in the last of the Minis. Fuel injection and catalytic converters were added, before the last of these engines was built in 2000, ending 49 years of production. As track records go, the little engine had done very well indeed.

after more than fifty years of production, leaving the upmarket Allegros with nowhere to go.

Increasingly at odds with the rest of the Austin Morris range, it didn't make sense in anybody's book to move production to yet another factory. So, this old-fashioned yet charmingly eccentric model disappeared from the showrooms, leaving the Vanden Plas name to become nothing more than a trim level on Austins, Rovers and Daimlers. Almost 12,000 Allegro-based VPs were built; a relatively small number, but enough to ensure that this model paid its own way until the very end.

TOP MARKS

The year 1980 also saw radical changes to another long-lived aspect of the Allegro range: the A-series engine. Helping to give the 1100 and 1300 models credibility and dependability, this tough little unit certainly had an impressive track record. Its remarkable ability to cope with increasingly more demanding applications (the weight of the 1,098cc Marina van has pushed its pulling power to the limit), plus the engine's revvy nature, made it a multi-purpose powerplant.

With little money to develop a new engine, Austin Morris had earmarked the useful A-series for use in the forthcoming Metro (briefly named the Mini-Metro due to legal reasons). Despite its strengths, though, it was clear that serious development was in order to help this ageing, push-rod-powered design remain competitive during a new decade. As a result, the unit was thoroughly re-worked. Stronger, better-balanced crankshafts

All except the base model featured this 'soft touch' plastic steering wheel, fitted with an Austin Morris badge towards the end of production. Although an ergonomic improvement, it lacked the character of the earlier thin-rimmed wheel, or the hilarity of the infamous quartic item.

In time-honoured tradition, the more money you paid, the more switches you got. A rear fog-lamp was always fitted, but the number of blank spaces varied from model to model.

and connecting rods were joined by a stiffer engine block and numerous other small improvements.

Externally, the old SU HS4 carburettors were ousted in favour of the more efficient SU HIF 38 and HIF 44 designs, while the manifolds were improved, the exhaust gaining a double down-pipe.

Painted red with a black rocker cover, instead of the all-black coating used on the old A-series, and adorned with an improved air-filter, the old engine had certainly been given a boost. To celebrate, rocker cover stickers were fitted bearing the unit's snappy new name, 'A-Plus'.

Rationalization was still Austin Morris' watch word, meaning that whatever engines the new Metro got, the Allegro would also benefit from. So, with the Metro's 1980 launch date looming, the last

stocks of A-series engines were used up before the new A-Plus units were substituted on the Allegro assembly lines.

This was good news for the 1.3 Allegros. The A-Plus continued the 1275cc capacity, meaning that a straight swap was easy. Thanks to the new engine's more efficient breathing and carbure-tion, plus a helpful boost in the compression ratio, power for the 1275cc unit shot up from 54bhp to 62bhp. Things were not so good for the 1.1 Alle-gros, however.

Previously, the most basic Allegros had shared the 1098cc A-series with the Mini Clubman, thus keeping engine production figures at a healthy level to ensure the unit's survival. However, the Clubman was deleted in favour of the new Metro range, which

By the end of the Allegro's life, engine size no longer dictated trim specification. Taking the lead at the Allegro's fortieth-anniversary celebrations at the Heritage Motor Centre, this late 1.3 HLS was equipped and trimmed to exactly the same standard as the 1.5 HLS, as well as the range-topping 1.7 HLS. Earlier 'High-Line' models also featured vinyl roofs.

only used 998cc and 1275cc capacity engines. Rather than creating, at great cost, a 1.1 A-Plus exclusively for the end-of-life Allegro, the latest 998cc engine was slotted beneath ADO67's bonnet.

Due to the 998cc A-Plus engine's efficiency, power only fell slightly for the cheapest Allegros, down to a modest 44bhp. However, although ideally suited to the Metro and the surviving Minis, this smaller, less torquey engine had its work cut out in the heavier Allegro. Austin Morris glossed over the slight reduction in performance in its sales literature, promoting the new 1-litre model on the benefits of its fuel economy.

3-STYLE

More changes were in store for the Allegro. Curiously, the model designations across the entire range were re-distributed, with several detail changes to different models. To the casual observer, this was nothing short of confusing. What had

been the HL models were now designated HLS, with the L models tagged HL, and the basic 1.3 becoming the 1.3L. To disguise the reduction in engine size for the cheapest variant, the gap previously occupied by the 1.1 was now filled with the 998cc L.

What's more, the previous lack of any kind of badges was now made up for with a smattering of the Austin Morris logos. One was fitted to the otherwise featureless front grille, with another on the steering wheel and a third on the boot-lid. The script for the rear badges was also revised: gone was the brushed aluminium, to be replaced by cut-out chrome-effect plastic lettering. The round, indicator side-repeater lamps, which had resembled the old BL roundel, were gone in favour of rectangular items. The range-topping models also lost their vinyl roofs.

Inside, all manual transmission models were now equipped with the Metro's black 'pool ball' type of gear lever knob, labelled with the pattern for

Orange is clearly an indication of high status. The interior of the very last-of-the-line **HLS** model was awash with ribbed velour, laid across redesigned front seats. Head-rests and black-topped door cards were standard. Intriguingly, the Allegro wasn't alone with this trim; similar treatment was given to the upmarket **Metro** and **Morris Ital.** BMIHT

When the versatile Metro arrived on the scene, Austin-Rover's small-car range was given a much-needed shake-up. The Mini was demoted to an economy special, while the Triumph Acclaim's arrival made the poor old Allegro look a bit out-classed. BMIHT

AUSTIN ROVER

MAESTRO 1.3HLE
BRITAIN'S MOST ADVANCED ECONOMY CAR

The Maestro took over where the Allegro left off, albeit swapping the Hydragas and saloon bodies for conventional springs and a hatchback. Despite Allegro production ceasing in 1982, there was enough unsold stock to tide dealers over until the Maestro's 1983 launch. BMIHT

four or five gears, depending upon which gearbox was used. The seat covers were given yet another change in stitching patterns. Beige 'Marle' cloth featured throughout the interiors of the L models, with the HL variants using a black version of this material. For both of these trim levels, the heat-pressed vinyl door-trims now featured black upper sections, regardless of the overall interior colour scheme. The arm rests were also now available only in black, while the estates gained rubbing strips to the floor of their load bays.

The interior of the HLS had changed somewhat, too. The head-rest-equipped seats were now covered in bright orange velour, with ruffled sections let into the covers. Ribbed door-trims, in matching orange, were complemented by the colour

co-ordinated carpet. It was certainly a very distinctive package and matched the interiors of the plushest models from the Metro and Morris Ital ranges. Black plastic door-pockets eventually worked their way on to the specifications sheets. However, this was the final form that the Allegro would take, until its demise.

By 1982, the new Austin Maestro was just around the corner. A launch date of spring 1983 had been set, and British Leyland had high hopes, as had been the case with the launch of the Allegro a decade earlier. However, the specification for the new family car looked to be bang-on the money. A five-door hatchback body was a good move, in light of the hatch-equipped Ford Escort Mk3 and Vauxhall Astra.

Conventional coil-spring suspension and neutral styling, penned by David Bache and Harris Mann, would eliminate several of the criticisms of its forerunner. With a choice of 1.3 A-Plus or 1.6 R-series engines, the Maestro could work together with its smaller Metro sibling. With any luck, these two Austins could snatch victory from the jaws of defeat, as BL entered another challenging decade of trials and tribulations.

THE END

In March 1982, production of the Austin Allegro ceased. The small resurgence in sales the ADO67 design had experienced during its later years had well and truly fizzled away. Although a full year before its Maestro replacement would go on sale, the backlog of unsold dealer stock ensured that the small number of new Allegro buyers wouldn't go wanting.

Altogether, 667,192 examples had been built during its nine-year production life. There had been a few highs and plenty of lows for the little Austin along the way. It never proved itself to be a great car but there were moments when the Allegro seemed to be developing into a good one. There's no escaping the fact that its inability to even rival the 2,151,007 production total of the ADO16 1100/1300 was a disappointment. However, regardless of its unsuccessful life, the Allegro's afterlife would prove to be much more remarkable.

Of all Allegro models, the final incarnation makes the most sense today as an everyday classic. It may lack the design quirks and lurid colour schemes of earlier versions, but its heavily revised mechanicals mark the Allegro 3 out as a competent car to drive.

Technical Specifications
Austin Allegro 3, 1.0-litre model, A+ engine, 1980–82

Layout and chassis   Two-door/four-door saloon with all-steel unitary construction body

Engine
Type	BLMC 4-cylinder in-line
Block material	Cast iron
Head material	Cast iron
Cylinders	4-cylinder in-line
Cooling	Water
Bore and stroke	64.58 × 76.32mm
Capacity	998cc
Valves	Overhead valve, two valves per cylinder
Compression ratio	9.6:1
Carburettor	Single SU type HIF 38
Max. power (DIN)	44bhp@5,250rpm
Max. torque	71.7lb ft@3,000rpm
Fuel capacity	10.5 gallons (47.7 litres)

Transmission
Gearbox	Four-speed manual, synchromesh on all forward gears	
Clutch	Single dry plate, diaphragm spring type	
Ratios	1st	3.647:1
	2nd	2.185:1
	3rd	1.425:1
	4th	1.000:1
	Reverse	3.667:1
Final drive	4.33:1	

Suspension and steering
Front	Independent by unequal length suspension arms, trailing tie rods and by gas- and fluid-filled 'Hydragas' displacer units, interconnected front to rear
Rear	Independent by trailing arms and by gas- and fluid-filled 'Hydragas' displacer units, interconnected front to rear
Steering	Rack-and-pinion
Tyres	145-13 radial
Wheels	13in, pressed-steel disc, bolt-on
Rim width	4.5in

Brakes
Type	Servo-assisted hydraulic, front discs, rear drums with leading/trailing shoes
Size	9.68in discs front; 8in drums rear

Dimensions

Track	
Front	53.62in (1,362mm)
Rear	53.70in (1,364mm)
Wheelbase	96.14in (2,442mm)
Overall length	151.67in (3,852.5mm)
Overall width	63.52in (1,613.4mm)
Overall height	55.04in (1,398mm)
Unladen weight	1,794lb (814kg) two-door
	1,838lb (834kg) four-door

Performance

Top speed	80mph (128km/h)
0–60mph	19.6sec

Technical Specifications

Austin Allegro 3, 1.3-litre model, A-series engine (A+ engine), 1980–82

Layout and chassis   Two-door/four-door saloon or two-door estate with all-steel unitary construction body

Engine

Type	BLMC 4-cylinder in-line
Block material	Cast iron
Head material	Cast iron
Cylinders	4-cylinder in-line
Cooling	Water
Bore and stroke	70.64 × 81.28mm
Capacity	1275cc
Valves	Overhead valve, two valves per cylinder
Compression ratio	8.8:1/9.4:1
Carburettor	Single SU type HS4/Single SU type HIF 44
Max. power (DIN)	54bhp@5,250rpm/62.7bhp@5,600rpm
Max. torque	64.74lb ft@3,000rpm/72lb ft@3,100rpm
Fuel capacity	10.5 gallons (47.7 litres)

Transmission

Gearbox	Four-speed manual, synchromesh on all forward gears (optional four-speed automatic)	
Clutch	Single dry plate, diaphragm spring type	
Ratios	1st	3.525:1/3.647:1
	2nd	2.218:1/2.185:1
	3rd	1.433:1/1.425:1
	4th	1.000:1/1.000:1
	Reverse	3.544:1/3.667:1
Final drive	3.938:1/3.765:1	

Suspension and steering

Front	Independent by unequal length suspension arms, trailing tie rods and by gas- and fluid-filled 'Hydragas' displacer units, interconnected front to rear
Rear	Independent by trailing arms and by gas- and fluid-filled 'Hydragas' displacer units, interconnected front to rear
Steering	Rack-and-pinion
Tyres	155-13 radial
Wheels	13in, pressed-steel disc, bolt-on
Rim width	4.5in

Brakes

Type	Servo-assisted hydraulic, front discs, rear drums with leading/trailing shoes
Size	9.68in discs front; 8in drums rear

Dimensions

Track	
Front	53.62in (1,362mm)
Rear	53.70in (1,364mm)
Wheelbase	96.14in (2,442mm)
Overall length	151.67in (3,852.5mm) saloons
	155.22in (3,942.6mm) estate
Overall width	63.52in (1,613.4mm)
Overall height	55.04in (1,398mm) saloons
	55.80in (1,417.3mm) estate
Unladen weight	1,876lb (851kg) estate
	1,794lb (814kg) two-door
	1,838lb (834kg) four-door

Performance

Top speed	84mph (135km/h)/84mph (135km/h)
0–60mph	18.4sec/18.1sec

CHAPTER FIVE

BUYING AND OWNING AN ALLEGRO

DARK DAYS

The decades that followed the end of Allegro production were almost as tumultuous as those during its heyday. As an outdated and thoroughly unfashionable car, the surviving Allegros lingered on as cheap transportation for those with shallow pockets. With a total lack of desirability keeping values low, many were bought for a pittance, driven into the ground and then thrown away. This was no different to countless other forgotten cars of the past.

However, the Allegro was never truly forgotten. Its appalling reputation in the eyes of the public,

This is the age-old view of the Allegro: an unreliable old shambles. However, this needn't be so. Buy a good example and look after it, and its reliability will astonish you. This neglected Allegro 3 was suffering from a faulty alternator and a tired battery.

whether deserved or not, never faded. The model had become a symbol of all that had been wrong not just with British Leyland, but also the militant and strike-plagued 1970s as a whole. The competence of the later models may have been swiftly forgotten but the infamy of those early, quartic steering wheel-adorned versions, which were troubled by reliability and build-quality problems, ensured that the Allegro was remembered, while other cars disappeared into obscurity.

As a scapegoat for the media, desperate to find 'the world's worst car' to ridicule, the strangely shaped Allegro was perfect. Top Gear's Jeremy Clarkson famously knocked over an up-ended Vanden Plas 1500, using a Morris Marina suspended by a crane, as part of a giant game of pub skittles. A beige Allegro saloon was driven in the *One Foot in the Grave* television series by a character devoid of street cred or style. If a cheap or undesirable 1970s car was needed for a TV production, the chances are that an Allegro would be found. It was a car stuck in the cultural doldrums.

ALLEGROS UNITE

However, as we've already seen, the Allegro still had much to commend it. Its strengths as a usable, comfortable small car, coupled with absurdly low purchase and running costs, meant that many soldiered on for years as everyday transport. The cars

That's better. A well-maintained Allegro can be relied upon to jump-start lesser vehicles with flat batteries, such as this poorly Land Rover Discovery. The willingness to start of the A-series versions in particular makes them ideal for winter motoring.

Be wary when searching for an Allegro to buy. Not only has this snow-covered car been abandoned outside for some time, it has a pronounced list to one side. This is as a result of a damaged Hydragas displacer; not quick or easy to replace.

that had been the victims of British Leyland's wildly varying build quality had long since disappeared, leaving the best examples to provide simple, economical motoring.

What's more, many of these 'good' examples proved themselves to be surprisingly reliable. The simple, rugged A-series engines, in particular, were almost indestructible, while Alex Moulton's Hydragas suspension was both reliable and rugged. Long-term rust-resistance proved to be remarkably good, especially compared to its rot-prone ADO16 forerunner. With handling that was entertaining and safe, these bargain-basement Austins started to make a lot of sense to those 'in the know'.

Then, in 1989, something extraordinary happened, which would change the fortunes of the Allegro forever. As part of a wearisome joke, an unknown hoaxer contacted a number of classic car magazines, claiming to be setting up an Austin Allegro owner's club. After all, who would join an organization for such an unloved car? However, this joke backfired to an astonishing degree.

When word got out that such a club was being formed, a remarkable number of individuals expressed an interest in joining. The classic car world may have been wary of these maligned machines but it appeared that there were plenty who were keen to extol the Allegro's overlooked virtues. An enthusiastic Allegro owner, Lynne Marshall, stepped forward to found a genuine Allegro club. By early 1990, the Allegro Club International had been created, bringing owners and enthusiasts together. Ever since, this welcoming and forward-looking club has matched its desire to further the Allegro's cause, with a refreshing approach to never take itself too seriously.

This Vanden Plas 1500 looks much more promising from a distance, but beware. Closer inspection reveals serious rust beneath that shiny paint. Some of the interior trim is damaged too, which will be costly to restore or replace.

This estate is a much better proposition. Although cosmetically scruffy, with obvious repair work to the nearside front wing, its otherwise straight and unmolested condition is far preferable to a heavily bodged car.

STYLE ICON

By the beginning of the new millennium, the styles, colours, clothes, furniture and – most crucially – cars of the 1970s were back in fashion. Having represented everything that had been bad about the decade, the Allegro was suddenly regarded as an icon of the era, regarded with nostalgia. Its reputation was still well known but, if anything, this only made the car more fascinating to a whole new generation. Its role as a police panda car in the hugely popular *Life on Mars* television series in 2006, set in 1970s Manchester, only cemented this further.

Experiencing a surge in popularity as a quirky and inexpensive retro classic, the Allegro had finally come of age, as an accepted member of the classic car community. Many examples had already perished during the car's twilight period, though.

In 2013, the DVLA had only 291 roadworthy examples on its books, although a great deal more lingered on in barns, garages and on driveways.

As a result, what was once a common sight on British roads is now much scarcer. However, the attrition rate for cars of the 1970s and 1980s on the whole has tended to be higher than, say, those from the 1960s, which were regarded as items to be cherished much earlier on in their lives. Compared to many of its period rivals and British Leyland-built contemporaries, which have disappeared in vast numbers, the Allegro hasn't done too badly.

All of this means that, as the Allegro begins its fifth decade, there has arguably never been a better time to buy a member of the ADO67 family. If you're searching for an enjoyable and affordable family classic, then look no further.

Keep your head if looking at an Allegro that has been in dry storage. Although a good way to find a car with a solid body, bear in mind that a car that hasn't been used for months, or even years, will need re-commissioning. Rubber items, such as tyres, hoses, fuel pump diaphragms, will be ripe for replacement, while the brakes are likely to be seized.

'Buy the best example you can afford' is time-honoured advice, but it still holds up today. With Allegro prices far lower than the majority of classic cars, it will pay in the long-term to seek out the right car and spend a little more on it.

HOW TO BUY THE BEST ALLEGRO

The days of low-mileage, near-immaculate Allegros changing hands for a pittance are long gone. Now, the Allegro is – quite rightly – regarded with a great deal of affection by a loyal band of followers. Demand is much stronger than it was during the car's 'banger' era, so you're unlikely to find a half-decent example of this 1970s icon being given away, as was once the case.

However, although no longer absurdly cheap, the Allegro still represents outstanding value in the classic car world. There are still a number of classic saloons and estates that can be inexpensively purchased and run on a tight budget. There are also classics that offer real-world usability. However, few can rival the Allegro's compromise between low-cost and everyday practicality, making it a smart choice for those looking for a characterful, yet pocket-friendly, everyday classic.

Despite gradually snowballing in popularity in recent years, most Allegros offered for sale still command relatively modest prices. Compared with other commendable small classics, such as the Ford Anglia 105E, Morris Minor and even the Allegro's predecessor, the BMC 1100/1300, asking prices for the ADO67 are still consistently low.

Sure, there are exceptions to the rule. The high-specification Vanden Plas derivatives consistently demand a premium over the normal Austin-badged Allegros. While project VPs still change hands for

Low mileage often means good condition, but this isn't always the case; an Allegro used only for the occasional short journey won't have had time to warm its engine through, causing premature wear. Buy according to condition, rather than the odometer reading.

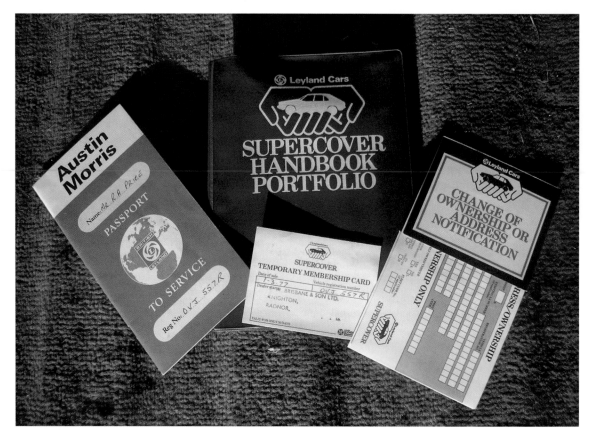

Original paperwork is always highly desirable, proving a car's provenance and history. **A BL Supercover handbook or 'Passport to Service,' as shown here, is a prized find indeed.**

Dealer window stickers are another charming indication of an Allegro's past life. This estate still wears the promotional rear tail-gate sticker of the garage to which it was originally supplied.

Obtaining a spares'
car can be an
excellent way to
save money on
replacement parts,
provided you have
the space (and
understanding
neighbours!).
This badly rotten
Allegro 3, home
to a considerable
number of spiders
and mice, yielded
many trim,
electrical and
mechanical parts.

If you own an Allegro, you can rest assured that the Allegro Club International is always there for help and support in keeping your car on the road. The benefits aren't merely practical: the ACI is one of the most welcoming and friendly classic car clubs out there.

little money, excellent examples can command anything up to £3,000. Rare Allegros, such as the Equipe, early 1750 models and the Crayford convertible, are a different story. These crop up for sale so rarely it is almost impossible to place a value on them.

However, the conventional models still offer outstanding value. In general, Series 1 models are worth fractionally more than examples of the Allegro 2, which are in turn more valuable than the Allegro 3 models. Although deleted early in the car's lifetime, the quartic steering wheel is seen by many as being a quintessential part of the Allegro experience; having one fitted is always a selling point. Regardless, with a little searching, solid, roadworthy examples can still be secured for less than £1,000.

Another feather in the Allegro's cap is the availability of parts. Although it should be noted that the supply of spares certainly does not rival that of, say, the classic Mini, for which almost every component can be purchased new, the Allegro still compares favourably with the majority of popular classics.

Thanks to the efforts of the Allegro Club International in running a spares' supply scheme, keeping any Allegro on the road is a realistic prospect. If a replacement part cannot be secured through the club, then its members will know of somebody who can supply the desired item. A handful of independent parts supply companies also offer a wide range of remanufactured Allegro parts, such as engine, braking, transmission and electrical components.

Second-hand parts, as well as unused 'new old stock' period replacements, regularly change hands at autojumbles and through internet auction sites. Fortunately, British Leyland's policy of sharing components across a number of models is a real boon to the twenty-first century Allegro owner. Look across the corporation's range of models – Mini, Maxi, Princess, Marina, Metro – and with a bit of detective work, you'll find components shared with the Allegro.

The greatest benefits of this parts' inter-changeability can be experienced by owners of 998cc, 1098cc and 1275cc A-series and A-Plus powered cars. Variations on these powerplants were famously used in the Mini, Morris Minor and MG Midget; fortunately each of these is supported by an extensive network of parts specialists. Sourcing a replacement part for one of the smaller-engined Allegros should not be a problem.

The reasons for buying an Allegro are not purely financial, though. As we've already discussed, the ADO67 design has much to offer in terms of road-holding and comfort. Don't let the variable build-quality put you off. The general rule of thumb is that, if an Allegro has survived for this long, then it's 'one of the good ones'. Buy a roadworthy car in good condition that has been used regularly by the previous owners and the chances are that most of the likely problems associated with age or lack of use will have long been sorted.

Flying the flag for the Allegro; most owners enter into the spirit of fun that accompanies these cars. Few classics encourage such a light-hearted attitude from their drivers.

BUYER'S CHECKLIST: WHERE TO LOOK

Bodywork

Although the Allegro is more rust-resistant than many of its contemporaries (including its fore-runner, the 1100/1300), the youngest example is still over thirty years old. This is more than enough time for rain, road salt and mud to have helped rust leave its mark on the bodywork. Bodywork condition should be the most important factor when assessing a car for sale.

Start by inspecting the front wings. These typically rot from the inside out above the indicator units [1] due to mud and debris trapping moisture here. Check their lower front corners and where they meet the front panel [2]; this seam corrodes. The front panel itself is also susceptible along its bottom edge. Evidence of filler here could suggest repairs or attempts to hide rot. Allegro 3 models are more difficult to inspect here, due to the fitment of the plastic front spoiler. Unused replacement wings are relatively easy to track down. Look out for holes in the front corners of the bonnet.

It should be easy to spot rust on the scuttle panel, beneath the windscreen [3]. Moisture is typically trapped beneath the lower corners of the windscreen rubber seal, leading to the inevitable bubbling beneath the paintwork. Corrosion here

The mismatched areas of paintwork make identifying past repairs easy on this estate. The rot spots you should pay particular attention to inspect are: [1] front wings above the sidelamps, [2] lower front wings and tie-bar mounts, [3] front scuttle below the windscreen, [4] lower front-wing corners, [5] jacking points and sill edges, [6] inner rear wheel-arches and lips, [7] rear valance, [8] boot-lid/ tail-gate and door lower edges.

The four jacking points will typically look like this: dented brackets, with surface rust and missing underseal. Inspect the steel they are welded to; this is a rot-prone area. Later literature insists on jacking from the end of the sill, rather than the rear jacking point.

is typical; if the car you're looking at is solid here, then it is one of the lucky ones. With the bonnet up, look for signs of rust around the front Hydragas suspension sphere mounts, and also where the flat tops of the inner wings meet the bulkhead; holes here are not uncommon.

A plastic splash-guard is screwed into position at the rear of the inner wheel-arch [4], although if this is broken or missing, the vertical rear edge of the wing will have suffered from road spray, as will the front end of the sill panel. Rot can take hold around mountings for aerials and indicator repeater lights, as well as in the lip of the outer wheel-arch. Underneath the car, look at the brackets for the tie bars, bolted on to the front suspension. Forty years of winter road salt is likely to have weakened this area.

Pay close attention to the four jacking points [5], which are typically rusted out due to caked-

on mud and damaged underseal. The rear jacking-points can trap moisture, rotting out the floor pan above them; lift the carpet beneath the rear seat to inspect this area from above. A square bracket, designed to help locate the original design of scissor-jack, is often flattened or missing if a trolley jack has frequently been used. Interestingly, British Leyland stated that the rear jacking-point was not to be used for jacking; instead, the jack should be located securely beneath the rearmost end of the sill structure.

Next, cast your eye along the sills. These box sections, running along the sides of the car, are critical to the strength of the body shell. On most Series I models, these are helpfully left bare, which eases inspection. If any repair work has been carried out, satisfy yourself that it has been done to a reasonable standard. As Allegro values were

The seam where the front panel and front wings meet is another rot spot. Check this carefully for signs of filler, as well as above the front side-lamp units; bubbling here is the norm, rather than the exception.

rock-bottom for so long, many examples will have seen hasty patch repairs to bodge the car through another MoT.

On later cars, sill trims were fitted as standard, which makes inspection much trickier. Bubbling on the door steps around these panels is a clue to corrosion beneath, while lifting the edge of the carpets is essential to assessing the inner sill. If the rivets or plastic retaining clips have been replaced by screws, ask the vendor if the sill trim has been removed for repairs. The floors may have deteriorated around their edges, particularly if a there is a window-seal leak.

An underside that is liberally coated in protective wax suggests that the owner has taken care to protect their car from rust. Beware thick, black underseal, however; there's no telling what might lie underneath it. The rear wheel-arches [6] can also harbour corrosion at their innermost points, as well as their outer lips.

Take a look at the rear valance [7]. On saloons, this is easily inspected from inside the boot and within the spare-wheel well on estates. Being vulnerable to stone chips and winter salt, these panels frequently develop holes, particularly around the rearmost exhaust system mount, on the panel's nearside.

Move your attention to the door bottoms, as well as the lower edges of the boot-lid or tailgate [8]. As the window seals age and the door drainage-holes get blocked, trapped moisture rusts its way out. Fortunately, these panels are bolted to the body shell and are also easy to track down second-hand. However, if these panels are in a bad way, don't expect the car's main structure to have fared much better.

Panel fit should be reasonably good and all doors should open and close easily. Be on your guard for accident damage if this isn't the case. It's a similar story with the boot-lid – again, these rust and are easy to replace, although estate tail-gates may take some tracking down.

External trim on the Allegro is generally simple and hardy. Rusted bumpers, as well as grilles, badges and hubcaps for most of the Allegro models, are easy to replace with good second-hand parts. However, the Vanden Plas derivatives feature addi-

tional wheel trims, as well as unique hubcaps, which can go missing. Also pay close attention to that imposing Vanden Plas grille; having a damaged item repaired won't be cheap, making replacement a much more economical prospect.

The plastic bumper end cappings of the Allegro 3 frequently get damaged or fall off, and may prove elusive to replace, particularly for higher spec models with silver inserts. Also, this model's plastic wheel-trims and wheel-nut covers are easily damaged. These were also shared with the last Maxi models but are not that easy to track down.

Engine

Although a complete service history is highly desirable, don't assume that the Allegro you're looking at will have such complete documentation.

Regardless of whether you're looking at an A- or E-series Allegro, carry out the same under-bonnet checks. Check [1] the oil at the dip stick for its colour and under the oil-filler cap for 'mayonnaise', [2] the colour of the coolant and condition of the hoses and radiator core, [3] signs of carburettor leaks or perished fuel hosing, [4] leaks from the brake and clutch master cylinders, [5] the function of all electrics and health of the charging system.

PLUGS-RN9YC - 0.024
          RN9YCC - 0.032
POINTS - 0.015
TAPPETS - 0.011
FR/ORD - 1342
TYRES
   F - 26 lbs
   R - 24 lbs

Some past owners may have left visual clues to a car's maintenance, such as the technical data painted on the underside of this bonnet. Stickers dating the most recent service also suggest that a maintenance regime has been maintained.

Not only are these old cars but many of these little Austins have served their time as ultra-cheap everyday transport, whose owners would have been less concerned by keeping the car's paperwork updated. As a result, it is vital that you thoroughly inspect the car you're considering purchasing.

As we've seen, the 1100 and 1300 versions of the Allegro were fitted with the 1098cc and 1275cc versions of the A-series engine. These engines were eventually replaced for the last Allegro 3 models by the revised A-plus engine, in either 998cc or, as before, 1275cc capacities. All of these engines are tough and long-lived. It's a similar story for the 1485cc and 1748cc E-series units, with their all-iron construction and more relaxed nature.

However, an abused or heavily worn powerplant can't be expected to provide reliable, trouble-free service. Before the engine has been started, dip the oil. Ideally, the lubricant will be clean and golden; thick, tar-like oil clearly hasn't been changed for a very long time, promoting wear. Excessive fumes from the oil-filler bore when the engine is idling are a bad sign, suggesting excessive bore wear. Keep an eye open for traces of a white 'mayonnaise'-type substance on the dip stick or on the underneath of the engine oil-filler cap [1]. This is a sign that moisture has been mixing with the oil. A small amount may be due to the car having only been driven for short distances, preventing the engine from warming up sufficiently. Beware a large amount, as this suggests that water is getting into the engine's oilways, pointing fingers at the head gasket.

The engine should be reasonably eager to start and should be fairly quick to fire with a little choke. If it is particularly reluctant to start, then produces an excessive amount of white smoke from the exhaust, which does not clear, then all signs point to head-gasket failure. On A-series engines, changing this gasket is a straightforward task for the DIY mechanic to tackle. The timing chain for the overhead camshaft complicates matters slightly on the E-series engines, although a head-gasket swap is still within the reach of the competent home-mechanic.

Things get more complicated if the engine has been allowed to overheat, however. If the cylinder head has warped slightly, a machine shop can easily skim it flat. However, a warped block mating face requires engine removal and disassembly to rectify. Valve gear chatter isn't anything to worry about and could simply be that the valve clearances need re-adjusting; an easy DIY job.

Take a close look at the cooling system [2]. Early Allegros featured a metal coolant pipe halfway along

SU carburettors were fitted to all Allegros; if in good condition, these are reliable. Used widely on a range of British classics, replacements are easy to come by, as are brand-new servicing and rebuild kits.

the course of the radiator's bottom hose, whereas later models used a single rubber hose. Regardless, ensure that both the top and bottom hoses are not cracking or leaking, and that neither balloon under pressure; this points to imminent failure. The same goes for the rubber hoses that run to the heater.

Listen to the water pump while the engine is idling. A rumbling or squealing pump is nearing the end of its life, as is one that weeps coolant. The radiator core should be intact and free from debris, and certainly shouldn't be leaking. A radiator specialist can easily repair or recondition the unit, if required. Inspect the colour of the coolant in the radiator's expansion tank: brown, muddy water suggests that the coolant hasn't been changed in a long time.

The distributor is mounted low down on the front of the engine. Not only is it vulnerable to water ingress in wet weather, servicing the ignition gear tends to get neglected; ask when the points, condenser, rotor arm and distributor cap were renewed. Electronic ignition is fitted in this picture.

When up to temperature, the engine should run smoothly without the choke. Adjusting either the single or twin SU carburettors [3] is another easy DIY task, although a heavily worn, poorly operating unit could benefit from a rebuild or replacement. Fortunately, the SU carburettor was used on a wide range of classic cars and spares are easily available, as are brand-new replacement units. With the carburettors located directly above the hot exhaust manifold, ensure that the carburettor, or any of the pipes that feed it, are not dripping petrol. Drips from the mechanical fuel-pump, mounted on the rear of the engine, require immediate investigation.

Of course, even if the worst comes to the worst and you find yourself in possession of an Allegro with a sickly engine, this shouldn't be of too great a concern. With an abundance of parts and complete second-hand engines, not to mention the availability of rebuilt A-series engines from Mini specialists on an exchange basis, rebuilding or replacing your Allegro's powerplant shouldn't be a problem. However, the costs for such work quickly add up. Don't assume that spending significant amounts of money in this area will increase the overall value of the car by the same amount. Sadly, this is rarely the case.

Transmission

As with the engines themselves, the four-speed manual gearbox used on sub-1.3 litre Allegros is tough and long-lived. Mounted in the sump, it was also blessed with a particularly pleasant gear-change action, so cog-swapping should be an easy affair while on your test drive. Expect plenty of transmission whine while on the move; it is part of the cars' character. The unit's oil is shared with the engine, which is asking a lot of the lubricant. As a result, regular oil changes are essential in preserving the transmission.

The larger-engined E-series Allegros used a completely different five-speed gearbox, again mounted in the engine's sump. Although that extra gear is particularly useful in modern traffic, the gear-change itself was famously hit-and-miss. Don't expect changing gear to be a delight. That said, you should still be able to engage all gears without too much difficulty. Regular oil changes are also important to maintaining the health of this unit.

The power is transmitted to the front wheels by use of CV joints. Each of these is protected by a rubber boot. If this has split, the grease within the joint will be spilled out, allowing the joint to run

Most of the Allegro's consumables are widely available brand-new, from service items and brake parts to new clutch kits, as depicted here. Mechanical spares, which aren't available new, are usually easy to find second-hand or as New Old Stock.

The front hubs are fitted with these two grease nipples. The steering may feel stiff or heavy if these have not been greased at every service. The rubber boot covering the CV joint, shown here, can crack, spilling its grease and hastening the joint's demise.

dry and prematurely wear. Listen out for a tell-tale knocking noise while manoeuvring the car on full steering lock.

Due to the transverse location of the engine across the car, and the roominess of the engine bay, the clutch can be changed on both the A- and E-series engines without the need to remove the entire engine. This makes life simpler, if you are doing this job yourself, and helps to keep costs down, if you are paying for a garage to replace the clutch. New and new-old-stock clutch kits are also readily available. However, a tired clutch should still be a point for negotiation. If the unit only starts to 'bite' towards the top of the pedal's travel, or slips when warm, then replacement is imminent.

Be on your guard against faulty clutch hydraulics.

With the health of the hydraulics reliant upon rubber components, which are likely to be decades old, don't be surprised to find a cracked or perished flexible hose between the master and slave cylinders. The cylinders themselves may be leaking if their internal seals have decayed; watch out for weeping.

An ailing master cylinder will be given away by a trickle of clutch fluid in the driver's foot-well after use. Seal kits to rebuild the cylinders are available, as are replacement cylinders, although the latter tend to be costly. It is worth noting that the cylinders are different on the A- and E-series engines. Also, an A-series clutch slave cylinder may look the same as that fitted to a Mini, but be warned, the two parts are not interchangeable.

Simple, sliding, front-brake calipers are reliable but can partially seize if a car has been laid up for a while. Look out for cracking to the flexible brake hoses or rusty solid brake pipes; if these are perished, they must be renewed.

With the rear brake drum and wheel bearing carefully removed, access to the rear brake-shoes and cylinders is granted. The brake-shoe adjuster is at the top, with the wheel cylinder at the bottom; leaking or seizing of the latter spells replacement.

If you're inspecting a car fitted with an automatic gearbox, then be thorough with your test drive. The unit should be smooth and speedy with its ratio changes and kick down readily when the accelerator pedal is fully depressed. The four-speed gearboxes fitted to the Allegros were unusual in the automotive world for, like the manual versions, being mounted in the engine's sump and sharing its lubricant. It is especially critical that oil and filter changes have been carried out regularly; ask the owner when this was last done. A professional rebuild of one of these units will not be cheap.

Brakes

All Allegros had good brakes from the factory, with discs up front and drums on the rear. All but the cheapest early models came as standard with servo assistance [4], which lowers the pedal pressures required; this unit, incorporated into the master cylinder, is easily spotted while underneath the bonnet. Look at the bulkhead beneath the master cylinder: damage to the paintwork suggests that brake fluid has leaked out at some point. The Allegro 3 also features dual-circuit brake lines, effectively meaning that, if a pipe in one circuit is damaged, there will be enough pressure remaining in the other circuit to stop the car.

Regardless of the model, the braking system is generally reliable. This is, however, one area where a regularly used car will score over one that hasn't been driven for some time. Calipers and rear wheel-cylinders can stick if left dormant, noticeable if the car pulls to one side under braking. Fortunately, this isn't particularly difficult to rectify.

New wheel-cylinders can still be easily tracked down, while seal kits are available for the calipers;

alternatively, classic brake specialists can refurbish ailing examples. The rear wheel-cylinders and brake shoes can't be inspected without undoing the hub nut to remove the rear brake-drums. Instead, look out for any signs of fluid leakage on the brake backplates or the wheel rims.

If the flexible brake hoses look past their best, factor in new replacements; original-specification items are available, as are upgraded braided stainless steel pipes. Take a look at the steel brake lines for signs of corrosion; rust damage here is dangerous, and will compromise the safety of the car. Fortunately, corrosion-resistant copper brake-pipe sets are also available, ready made. Worn brake-pads and shoes are easily sourced, although if either of these has been allowed to wear down completely then the discs or drums may be scored.

Suspension and Steering

Fortunately, the Hydragas suspension, which was introduced with the Allegro, is generally reliable and rugged. As we've seen, this operates through interconnected pipes of fluid, while nitrogen-filled metal spheres do the job of damping. However, even this strong system can develop problems due to its age.

The first thing to note is whether or not the car sits level. Unlike a conventional suspension system, which can sag due to wear in metal components, the Hydragas system shouldn't have developed a list to one side. If the car you're looking at is noticeably lower on one side, then it could be due to one of two things.

First, some of the system's pressure could have leaked out over time. Provided there are no obvious leaks, it may be possible to rectify this with a pump-up using a specially-designed Hydragas pump. Due to the system's use in the Metro, as well as the later MGF sports car, most garages should still be equipped with such an item. Alternatively, ex-garage pumps can be bought second-hand.

If there is an obvious leaking of green fluid from beneath the car, then the system is clearly damaged. A split pipe is the most obvious cause, although a weeping displacer will need to be replaced. It is possible to repair the system at home, with the right know-how and tools, although enlisting the help of a British Leyland-friendly garage is a smart move.

In addition, the suspension ball joints can wear out, causing a knocking noise. Similarly, the front steering-swivels are equipped with two grease nipples each side; failure to keep these greased can lead to stiff steering. Otherwise, the rack and pinion steering system shouldn't cause any problems.

Electrics

The Allegro's electrical system [5] is fairly simple, with very little to go wrong. However, age can take its toll, so don't be surprised if not all of the electrics function perfectly. It is an old British car, after all. Poor earths and damaged wires, although simple problems to rectify, will probably account for at least one non-functioning component. The heated rear-window, which is likely to have had only occasional use, is one of the most common items to fail, as is the rear wash-wipe function on estates. Run through all of the dashboard switches to test for operation.

While testing the lights, one – or perhaps both – of the front side-lamps may fail to function. If a blown bulb isn't the culprit, the cause will almost certainly be a bad earth due to an excessively corroded lamp-base. These are attacked from behind by spray from the front wheels; it may be possible to clean up the unit to restore the earth, but replacement is the only cure for a badly damaged lamp.

With the engine running at idle, turn on the headlamps, followed by another electrical function, such as the wipers. If the engine stutters and the battery warning light comes on, expect either an ailing battery or a charging fault with the alternator. Fortunately, either problem is easy for the home mechanic to rectify. If additional accessories have been fitted, such as spot lamps or modern stereo systems, try to assess how neatly the job has been done. Bad wiring, with a clumsy mess of loose, ill-chosen wiring, could be a fire hazard.

Fortunately, most of the electrical parts were taken straight from the BL parts' bin; if you can't find the correct Allegro part, compare it to a Mini, Maxi, Marina or Princess item; it may be exactly the same.

A dead side-lamp usually means one thing: the rot-prone lamp unit has corroded, ruining the lamp's earth. Sometimes, cleaning with a wire brush can restore life to the unit. Not so here; the entire unit has fallen apart and filled with road dirt.

The Allegro's front-mounted radiator gave the distributor – mounted on the front face of both types of engine – better wet-weather protection than its forerunner the 1100/1300, as well as the Mini. However, in torrential rain storms and flash floods, they're not immune from the effects of a British winter. An old trick to keep moisture out of the distributor is to clothe it with an old rubber glove, with each finger cut to allow a HT lead to escape.

Interior

Some classic cars benefit from a wealth of trim parts being available from specialists. Sadly, the Allegro is not so lucky. What's more, the wide variety of colour schemes and patterns used can make finding direct replacements of trim pieces a tricky task. The carpets are moulded into shape and wear out, particularly the front items.

The same goes for seat covers, with cloth items being much less hardy than vinyl equivalents. Check

OWNER'S VIEW:
JENNY THURSTON

Serial Allegro-owner Jenny, with her husband Craig and friend Peter Simmonds, have carried out what is arguably the most thorough reliability test of the ADO67 design: a pan-European rally. Taking two weeks to visit fourteen countries, their steed of choice for this epic adventure was a hand-painted Allegro 2, sporting a 1275cc engine and mismatched panels. In common with many Allegro owners, Jenny has owned a multitude of these maligned Austins.

We started in Calais, then journeyed through France and Belgium, then into Germany. Next, it was down to Switzerland, through the north-east corner of Italy and up into Austria. From there, we went through Slovenia, Croatia and Serbia, spent a few days in Romania, dipped a toe into Ukraine, before heading back home to Norfolk, through Slovakia, Poland, Germany, Holland, Belgium, France.

We've done a few of these rallies in the past, and they're always great fun. Many people scrap their cars at the far end and fly home, but that's never been an option for us. Often the return journey home, when you don't really know where you'll be each night, is the best bit. Allegros are super cars for that sort of thing;

easy to fix, surprisingly capacious, economical and with readily available spares. And they evoke a hugely positive reaction, despite their unfortunate reputation. Almost without exception, the people we meet regard them with fond affection.

In our view, the Allegro now has a sort of rally pedigree. When you've taken them to such faraway places as Morocco, the Czech Republic and the Ukraine, you begin to feel there's not a lot they can't do.

Craig and I acquired our first Allegro when we were at university; we found it for sale for £200 and it appealed because it was cheap, British and something of an underdog. It was love at first sight. Ours was Russet brown and was my first experience of a classic car. Everything about it was so unusual, from the noise it made, to the smell of the interior. The people we met in the Allegro Club International were welcoming and incredibly helpful, and really kept us on the road during those early years.

That car turned out to be mostly made of filler, but we still have it, and it will have a proper restoration some day. Since then, things have snowballed. Almost before we knew it, we had eight of the things and were members of the Allegro Club International committee. There is something hugely lovable about an Allegro.

Don't be surprised if the interior trim is not original; it's often cheaper to replace badly damaged seats than to repair them. The Vanden Plas leather and wood trim is particularly sought after; here, it is fitted to a lowly 1.3L.

for splits and rips, and discolouration or decay on the rear seats' upright due to sun damage. Commonly used brown and black items can be found second-hand, but don't hold out much hope for the more luridly coloured items. The padding on the driver's seat bolsters is likely to be worn or sagging if the car has clocked up a particularly high mileage.

Dashboard tops also suffer from sun damage and commonly split. Again, sourcing a replacement from the correct model, in the correct colour, is likely to be a nightmare, unless you stumble across a scrapped car in the same colour scheme. Door trims are a similar story, often being butchered to fit aftermarket radio speakers. As a result, the condition of the interior should be almost as influential in your decision-making as that of the body and mechanicals.

Any damaged or missing trim will need to be replaced, which in turn will require plenty of searching. The Allegro Club International may be able to help track down certain items, such as seats and trim panels, although be prepared to start scouring autojumbles and internet auction sites for that elusive part. The BMC & BL Spares' Day rally

in Peterborough should be at the top of your list, along with the Beaulieu International Autojumble in Hampshire.

For the Vanden Plas models, the situation is even more awkward. Although the high-quality leather trim used on these cars is generally hard-wearing, repairing or re-trimming the seats is likely to be a costly exercise. The lacquer on walnut dashboards and door cappings can discolour and peel, if the wood has been allowed to get damp, and will not be cheap to put right. Again, replacement is the most cost-effective solution.

However, it is popular practice to upgrade a lesser Allegro using the interior trim from a scrapped VP. As a result, such fittings are sought after, and you'll probably have to fight to secure second-hand replacements. Curiously, the same goes for early Series I Allegros that have been parted from their original quartic steering wheels. This infamous part has become part of motoring folklore, making it something of a trophy for collectors of automobilia. With many quartic wheels now permanent decorations in such peoples' homes and garages, prices are high.

OWNER'S VIEW: RICHARD GUNN

Classic car journalist Richard Gunn is something of a champion for the humble Allegro. 'People often look surprised when I say I own one,' he admits. 'As a motoring journalist, surely I've driven thousands of vehicles, of all types and ages, over the years? Why would I want to own what is usually regarded as the worst British car ever made?

The truth is that, while Allegros may not have been the greatest things when they were new, as classic cars they're wonderfully entertaining and cheap to own. The ones that have managed to survive are the good ones, probably not built on a Friday afternoon in-between strike stoppages and then left out the back at Longbridge for six months.

I've owned eight over thirteen years, from basic lower powered models through to more performance-orientated, plusher examples, as well as the faux-Jaguar Vanden Plas variants. Every one of them has had a distinct and different personality. Some were utterly awful – like the automatic Series 3 that had no reverse – while others have been among the most reliable cars I've ever owned, capable of shrugging off the sort of abuse that would leave a much more expensive vehicle collapsed in a pool of oil.

All of these Allegros have been fun. They feel like bloated, roly-poly Minis that have consumed too many pies, yet still have a nice degree of bouncy handling and entertaining, lively performance about them. Most

revel in their 1970s fashion-victim status, painted in flamboyant oranges, yellows, turquoises and retina-searing greens or more insipid beiges and browns, with contrasting velour or vinyl interiors, occasionally decorated with peeling fake wood trim. It's like travelling back in time in a very low budget version of Dr Who's Tardis and discovering that the members of ABBA are that week's aliens.

Wherever you go in an Allegro, people will look and laugh. Sometimes, it's at you, but usually these days, it's with you. Time is a great healer and Allegros now have a cult classic status, as an icon of a time when Britain was a much simpler, less hectic place and our troubles seemed perhaps less serious than now. Often, you'll find these endearing Austins getting far more attention than much pricier and prestigious classics, because people can relate to them.

What's more, they must be among the cheapest ones around. The days of them being given away for free have pasted, but good examples can still be had for mere hundreds of pounds, and parts are still plentiful and inexpensive. They're so uncomplicated that most problems can be easily fixed by anybody with just a basic toolkit and some mechanical knowledge.

Allegros are comedy classics, able to raise a smile under most circumstances. Even when you're stranded by the side of the road waiting for the recovery services to arrive, they'll usually try to cheer you up by playing the Bay City Rollers at you from a tinny mono speaker. Mongrel-ish automotive charm really doesn't come much more endearing.

OWNER'S VIEW:
BEN WANKLYN

If I hadn't been given an Applejack green Allegro 3 in 2010, this book would undoubtedly never have been written. It was the third day on my new job with *Practical Classics* magazine, when I discovered that unloved machine loitering outside the magazine's workshop. Aside from its offensive colour, the poor thing had many other troubles. Its suspension had collapsed, owing to a blown Hydragas displacer, and its engine was both inoperative and non-original, having started life in a Metro. The interior was full of icy water and the nearside was sporting a number of dents. Its owner had emigrated and nobody wanted

the little Austin, not even for free. I offered to give it a good home.

A questionable decision by the magazine's features editor, to take the Allegro to the Essen motor show in Germany, saw it repaired and MoT'd. It rapidly became apparent that the smokey engine and groaning gearbox had been abused in a former life. However, friend Matt George and myself successfully completed the cross-Europe adventure in it, despite a dying alternator. Not even severe brake-failure on our way out of Germany, or an exploding tyre in Kent, could hold the Allegro back. Against all odds, our Applejack steed had performed impressively.

If a free, ropey Allegro could be so entertaining, how good could a decent one be, I wondered. A deliciously original Allegro 2 estate was purchased at the 2010 BMC & BL Spares' Day show in Peterborough. Utterly charming and huge fun to drive, I never looked back. Although rough around the edges, that estate became the only car I've ever owned never to break down. Ever. It would regularly jump-start lesser vehicles during the depths of winter. In a deeply regrettable decision, I eventually swapped that car for a DAF 33. We all make mistakes…

Two years later, I became the owner of a rust-free, low-mileage Allegro 3 that had spent many years in a motor museum. Russet brown and with leather Vanden Plas seats, it became my everyday car. However, it also taught me just how unreliable an Allegro can be. The steering, brakes, cooling system, clutch, clutch hydraulics, electrics, fuel system and much more, would take it in turns to fail or develop dangerous faults, despite near-constant maintenance and repairs. By the time I'd ironed out its faults, I'd fallen out of love with that car.

And my fourth Allegro? That was a hugely useful spares' car, bought while I was running my Russet brown example. Although terminally rusty and buried up to its wheel nuts in farmyard mud, it proved to be the smartest £50 I'd ever spent. I've had many Austin ups and downs, but then, so has the nation as a whole. Some Allegros were painfully bad cars, straight from the factory. Others were models of unfaltering reliability. But make no mistake, all were unforgettable for one reason or another.

INDEX

A-series engine   21, 31, 36, 51, 75, 116–8,
     129–30, 141–4
     803cc   15, 116
     848cc   20, 116
     948cc   17, 116
     998cc   116
     1071cc   116
     1098cc   23, 45, 47, 73, 101, 104, 107, 116, 137,
          142
     1275cc   24, 32, 45, 47, 74, 101, 107, 116, 119,
          137, 142
A-Plus engine   108, 116–9, 142–4
     998cc   104, 108, 116, 119–20, 137, 142
     1275cc   108, 116–7, 119–20, 122, 137, 142
ABBA   153
Abingdon   117
ADO16   21, 25–6, 31–2, 37, 40, 42, 45, 51, 53,
     57, 66, 72, 79, 123, 130, 133, 138, 149
     Austin 1100/1300   23–4
     Countryman/Traveller   24, 64, 76
     MG 1100/1300   23–4
     Morris 1100/1300   22–24, 57, 115–6
     Riley Kestrel   23–4
     Vanden Plas Princess 1100/1300   23–4, 59, 61,
          85, 115
     Wolseley 1100/1300   23–4
Alfa Romeo Alfasud   49, 66, 82
Allegro Club International   130, 136–7, 152
Alvis   27
Arab-Israeli war   57
Austin, Herbert   11
Austin 8   13
     1800/2200   24–6, 36, 61
     A30   15, 20, 105, 116
     A35   17, 20, 116
     A40/A50 Cambridge   16
     A40 Devon/Dorset   13, 15, 116

A40 Farina   17, 24–5, 77
A60 Cambridge   24, 27, 31, 36, 64
Allegro Equipe   80, 89–94, 100–2, 112, 136
Allegro Special LE   86
Ambassador   33, 37, 115
Kimberly/Tasman   25, 37
Maestro   33, 37, 99, 115, 117, 122–3
Maxi   45, 63, 66, 84, 108, 137, 141, 148
Metro   33, 35, 99, 105–6, 108, 115–23, 137,
     148
Metro Turbo   116
Montego   115, 117
Princess   33, 35, 39, 84, 137, 148
Seven   11–13, 114
Westminster   16, 115
Austin-Healey
     Sprite   19, 79, 116
Austin Morris   2 9, 31–2, 99–100
Autocar   40, 50, 53, 57
Automotive Products automatic
     transmission   21, 37, 47, 59, 81, 114, 117, 147

Bache, David   33, 123
Bay City Rollers   93–4, 153
BBC   40, 42, 57
Bertone   79
BMC Competitions Department   113
BMC Special Tuning   113
BMW Isetta   19
Bond Minicar   19
British Leyland   27–33, 41, 46, 53, 56–7, 83,
     99–102, 128, 137
British Motor Corporation   16–7, 20, 24, 26, 40,
     57, 61, 77
British Motor Holdings   27
B-series engine   24, 32
Burzi,   Dick 33

Chrysler   27, 30
C-series engine   36
Citroën, André   15, 20
Citroën   35–6, 89
  2CV   86
  GS   47, 82
  Traction Avant   15
  Visa   82
Clarkson, Jeremy   128
coal miners' strikes   56
Cofton Hackett   34
Commer   33
Completely Knocked Down kits   89, 91
Connolly leather   59–60
Connolly, Fred   57
Cowley   24, 33
Crayford   66, 136
CV joint   20, 144–5

Daimler   27, 118
  Double-Six   115
  DS420   115
Datsun
  120Y   81
  160B/180B   81
Downton   116
Dr Who   153
Duple   33
DVLA   131

E-series engine   29, 31, 34, 36–7, 53, 81, 141–4
  1485cc   45–6, 50, 59, 86, 114, 117, 142
  1748cc   47, 51, 114, 117, 142
E6 engine   37

Fiat
  124 Special   53
  128   45
Ford   21, 24–5, 30, 32, 49, 62, 66, 92, 107
  Anglia/Prefect 100E   16
  Anglia 105E   17, 33, 133
  Capri   33, 66
  Corsair   66
  Cortina   24, 31–3, 66, 81
  Escort   33, 45, 47, 81, 122
  Fiesta   81
  Zephyr/Zodiac Mk3   33

Fox, Roland   59
front-wheel   drive 20–21, 23, 30–31, 37, 81, 84
fuel injection   117

GKN alloy wheels   92, 94

Harriman, George   29, 37
Haynes, Roy   32–3
Hillman   62
  Avenger   45, 47, 49, 81
  Hunter   53, 81
Honda
  Civic   91
  Accord   91
Hopkirk, Paddy   25
Hydragas   31, 34–5, 42, 51, 84, 89, 109, 122,
    129–30, 139, 148
Hydrolastic   23–4, 30, 34–6, 38, 42, 51

Innocenti   77, 79–80
  Regent   79–80, 93–4
Issigonis, Sir Alec   19–21, 24–5, 28, 30–1, 36, 51,
    116

Jaguar   27, 60–1
  XJ12   57

K-series engine   117
King, Spen   36
Kingsbury, London   57, 115, 117

Land-Rover   27
  Discovery   129
  Range Rover   36
Leyland Australia   25, 37, 57
  Leyland P76   37, 57
Leyland Special Tuning   113
Life on Mars   131
London–Sydney Marathon   25
Longbridge   24, 33, 40, 77
Ludlow Fisher   29
Meadows Frisky   19
Messerschmitt KR175   19
Marbella, Spain   41–2
Metropolitan Police Panda cars   55–6
Lord, Leonard   1, 5–6, 19, 115
Leyland trucks   2, 7, 29, 36

Mann, Harris   8, 32–4, 36, 39, 53, 84, 93, 122
MG Car Company   16, 29, 86
  Magnette Mk IV   24
  MGB   57, 102, 106
  MGF   35, 148
  Midget   102, 116, 137
Mini   19–25, 44, 57, 66, 79, 89, 103, 112, 116–7,
  121, 136–7, 144, 146, 148–9
  Austin Mini Seven   20, 30
  Clubman   30, 43, 119
  Cooper 'S'   117
  Riley Elf   21
  Moke   21
  Morris Mini-Minor   19–20, 30
  van/pick-up   21
  Wolseley Hornet   21, 66
monocoque bodyshell   15, 24
Morris, William Richard   16
Morris   15–6, 20, 29–30, 32, 84
  1500 Nomad   37
  1800/2200   24–6, 36, 61
  Cowley   16
  Ital   33, 121–2
  Marina   28, 32–3, 35–6, 41–2, 66, 118, 128,
   148
  Marina Red Six   37
  Minor   15–19, 24–5, 27, 32, 41, 66, 133, 137
  Oxford Series   VI 24, 32, 36
Moulton, Dr Alex   23, 34, 36–7, 42, 130

Nanjing Automobile Group   115
National Enterprise Board   84
New Zealand Motor Corporation   91
Nitrogen   38
Nuffield Organisation   16
Nuffield, Lord   see Morris, William Richard

One Foot in the Grave   128
overhead camshaft   31, 37

Peugeot   66
  104   45
Pininfarina   17, 21, 24
Pressed Steel   27, 29

quartic steering wheel   7, 36, 44, 47, 53–6, 61–2,
  66, 73, 80, 118, 136, 152

R-series engine   122
Radiomobile   106
Raymond Loewy Company   33
Reliant Scimitar GTE   63, 65
Renault   36, 66, 81, 89
  4   82
  5   30, 45, 82, 94, 102
  12   82
  16   31, 47, 49, 53, 66, 82
Riley   16
  1.5   17
  4/72   24
Rolls-Royce   115
Rootes Group   25, 33
Rover   27, 118
  75   115
  SD1   33, 115

Seneffe, Belgium   89, 94, 102, 112
Simca 1100   45
Specialist Cars   29
Speedwell   116
Stage One tuning   113
Standard   27, 29
  Eight   16
Starsky and Hutch   94
Stokes, Donald   29, 38, 40, 62
SU carburettor   16, 45, 50, 52, 63, 77, 81, 94,
  114, 117, 119, 142–4
Suez Crisis   19
'Supervroom' advertising campaign   99–100
Swindon body plant   57

Talbot Sunbeam Ti   94
Technology, Ministry of   27
three-day week   56
transverse engine layout   20–1
Trentham paint shop   83
Triumph   27, 29
  Acclaim   121
  Dolomite Sprint   53
  Herald   17
  Stag   57
  TR7   33, 93
Turnbull, George   29, 32, 42

Vanden Plas   16, 57–61, 77, 85, 112, 114–5, 117–8

A120/A135   115
A105   115
Princess 3-Litre/4-Litre 'R'   115
Vauxhall   25, 30, 49, 62, 107
  Astra   122
  Chevette   81
  Victor   81
  Viva   45, 47, 81
Volkswagen   117
  Golf   66, 81, 94
  Passat   66

Polo   30, 81
Volvo   102
'Vroom Vroom' advertising campaign   87–8, 98

Webster, Harry   29, 34–5, 40
Wilson, Harold   27
Wilton carpet   59–60
Wolseley   11, 16, 84
  16/60   24, 36
  18/85/Six   24–5, 61
  1500   17

RELATED TITLES FROM CROWOOD

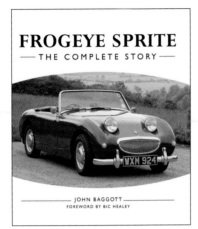

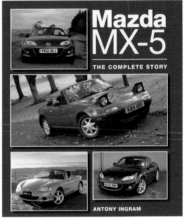

Frogeye Sprite
JOHN BAGGOTT
ISBN 978 1 84797 550 8
224pp, 280 illustrations

Lotus Elan
MATTHEW VALE
ISBN 978 1 84797 510 2
176pp, 250 illustrations

Mazda MX-5
ANTONY INGRAM
ISBN 978 1 84797 496 9
176pp, 200 illustrations

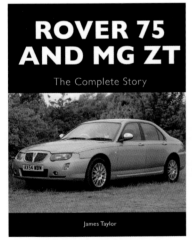

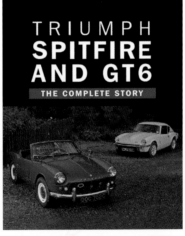

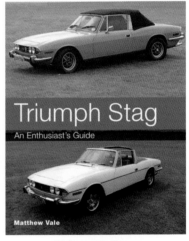

Rover 75 and MG ZT
JAMES TAYLOR
ISBN 978 1 84797 685 7
208pp, 270 illustrations

Triumph Spitfire and GT6
RICHARD DREDGE
ISBN 978 1 84797 703 8
176pp, 290 illustrations

Triumph Stag
MATTHEW VALE
ISBN 978 1 84797 735 9
144pp, 120 illustrations

In case of difficulty ordering, please contact the Sales Office:

The Crowood Press, Ramsbury, Wiltshire SN8 2HR UK

Tel: 44 (0) 172 520320   enquiries@crowood.com   www.crowood.com